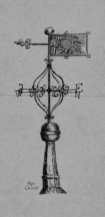

Rye
Church

CURIOUS
OBSERVATIONS
A COUNTRY MISCELLANY

❖

FROM THE PAGES OF
COUNTRY LIFE

CURIOUS OBSERVATIONS
A COUNTRY MISCELLANY

❋

FROM THE PAGES OF
COUNTRY LIFE

COUNTRY LIFE EDITOR MARK HEDGES

COMPILED AND EDITED BY SAM CARTER
SERIES CONSULTANT JOHN GOODALL

SIMON &
SCHUSTER
ILLUSTRATED

London · New York · Sydney · Toronto · New Delhi

A CBS COMPANY

First published in Great Britain by Simon & Schuster UK Ltd, 2011
A CBS COMPANY

1 3 5 7 9 10 8 6 4 2

SIMON & SCHUSTER
ILLUSTRATED BOOKS
Simon & Schuster UK Ltd
222 Gray's Inn Road
London
WC1X 8HB

www.simonandschuster.co.uk

Simon & Schuster Australia, Sydney

Simon & Schuster India, New Delhi

Series Editor and Project Manager: Sam Carter
Series Consultant: John Goodall
Country Life Picture Library Manager: Justin Hobson
Designer: Two Associates
Literary Agent: Jonathan Conway, Mulcahy Conway Associates

A CIP catalogue record for this book is available from the British Library

ISBN 978-0-85720-360-1

Printed and bound by CPI Group (UK) Ltd, Croydon, CR0 4YY

CONTENTS

"IT STARTED WITH A TITLE
THAT FALLS LIKE MUSIC UPON THE EAR,
OURS BEING AN ISLAND RACE
WHEREOF EVEN THE TOWN DWELLER
IS A COUNTRY MAN AT HEART . . ."

FOREWORD

W HEN THE FIRST issue of *Country Life* flopped off the printing press at 83–85 Southwark Street in January 1897, there was an ageing Queen Empress on the throne, whose empire was the biggest the world had ever seen. In a sense, the magazine was the indirect product of Victoria's love of the British countryside: her purchase of two great estates, Balmoral and especially Sandringham, which she bought to give her reckless son, the future Edward VII, something sensible to do with his time, had made the countryside and the country house fashionable.

Country Life was launched to help sell these now desirable country houses and estates. It also aimed to celebrate the life of the countryside in all its aspects, from field sports to farming and architecture to Arcadian idyll. From the first the magazine was luxuriously produced with exquisite illustrations and beautiful typography. As a novelty, it also made use of the technology to print photographs in half-tone. The venture succeeded brilliantly and over time *Country Life* has become more than just a highly successful weekly magazine, it has become a British institution.

Looking through past issues of *Country Life* is a dangerously beguiling pastime. On almost every page there are articles, letters or photographs that cry out for the casual reader's attention. This book, *Curious Observations: A Country Miscellany*, is a selection of these pieces. Their charm is partly bound up with the lost world they describe, but there is something timeless about some of the best contributions to the magazine. Gilbert White, the great Hampshire naturalist, said many people look, but few observe. Here are observations that collectively offer an insight into our national psyche: wry, witty and wonderful. In their own way, each one adds to the golden seam of what it is to be and to feel British.

MARK HEDGES
EDITOR OF *COUNTRY LIFE*
OCTOBER 2011

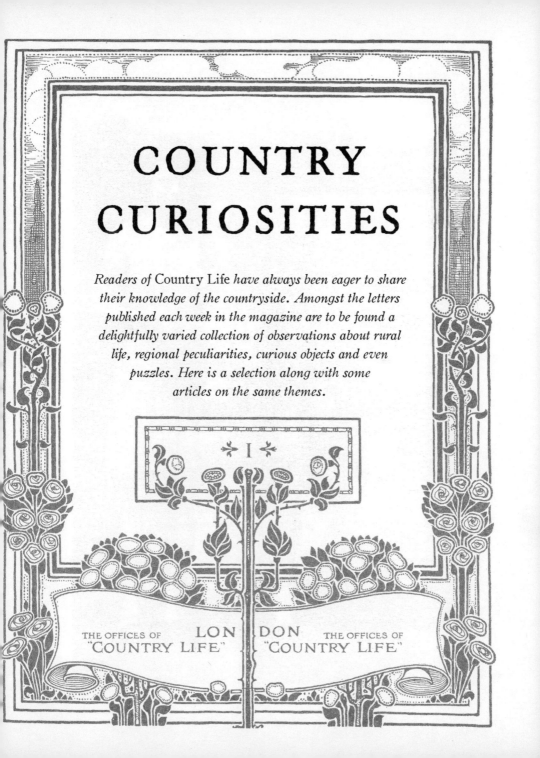

COUNTRY
CURIOSITIES

Readers of Country Life *have always been eager to share their knowledge of the countryside. Amongst the letters published each week in the magazine are to be found a delightfully varied collection of observations about rural life, regional peculiarities, curious objects and even puzzles. Here is a selection along with some articles on the same themes.*

❖ I ❖

THE OFFICES OF   LONDON   THE OFFICES OF
"COUNTRY LIFE"   "COUNTRY LIFE"

MARCH 26TH, 1938

A TRUANT'S TRIANGLE

TO THE EDITOR OF "COUNTRY LIFE."

SIR,—Native Shetland sheep show traits of character entirely out of harmony with the accepted traditions of the shepherd's gentle flock.

The sheep live on the common pasture-lands, and because of the bleak nakedness of the exposed hills during long periods they live somewhat precariously, always in search of food. The rugged nature of the country has made them goat-like in their nimble-footedness; and no opportunity of snatching a surreptitious mouthful from any protected crop is ever allowed to pass.

When summer comes and all arable lands are securely walled and fenced, these enclosures with their growing crops offer strong temptations to flocks exiled to close-cropped open hillsides. And perhaps it is the bolder, pioneering spirits in the flock who discover the possibility of leaping a wall or squeezing through a fence to the richer fields within. Certainly once one of these sheep discovers that a fence can be negotiated, it develops a technique which overcomes almost any fencing obstacle, and the only alternative left to the distracted occupier of the raided land is to subject the offender to the wooden triangle shown in the photograph, or to lead it to the slaughter-house. Sheep with wooden triangles on their necks are a common sight on Shetland hillsides.

No doubt it is a certain handicap to its wearer, but an inconvenience rather than cruelty, and perhaps an embarrassing humiliation to an enterprising explorer – but withal the lesser evil.—J. PETERSON

JANUARY 1ST, 1938

A POETICAL ESTATE

To the Editor of "Country Life."

Sir,—I send you photographs of two entertaining sign-posts in Cheshire. One is on the road from Budworth to Knutsford, and points the way to Arley Hall. The other, which amplifies in rhyme the more prosaic statement "Bridle road only," is near the Arley Hall drive. All the sign-posts on this estate are in rhyme.—W. Poole

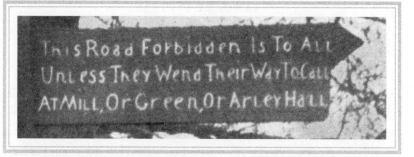

APRIL 10ᵀᴴ, 1942

A DOG-OPERATED
BUTTER CHURN

To the Editor of "Country Life."

Sir,—As an example of interesting things there may be mentioned a dog-operated butter churn, of which an illustration is enclosed. How long it may be since such a contrivance was used anywhere in England, I do not know, but many comparable churns were employed in North America less than 50 years ago and a few are still working on remote Welsh hill farms. I have also seen in a museum a dog treadwheel of the drum type, such as was used for turning a spit before an open fire. It may be pertinent to recall that Rowlandson's well-known sketch showing just such a wheel in use was made in South Wales. It was published in 1800. When dogs were last employed in kitchens for this purpose I do not know, but there is a record (unchecked) of Queen Victoria's having owned turnspit dogs in the 1840's, and other evidence also suggests that a few of these dogwheels were still used less than 100 years ago.—Countryman

AUGUST 10ᵀᴴ, 1940

A MOUSE-TRAP
THAT WILL NOT TAKE BIRDS

To the Editor of "Country Life."

Sir,—I was very much interested in your correspondent's letter about mouse-traps that will not catch birds when set in a garden. Undoubtedly the most effective and cheapest of these is the "Figure of Four" trap, which anyone can construct for himself with a pair of slates and three slivers of wood notched in the appropriate fashion. The trap has a hair-trigger setting; it is unaffected by any kind of weather; it is extremely deadly on mice; and it will not take birds. Not least among its advantages is that any taint of blood on the slates is simply washed off. I do not think there is a more deadly mouse-trap in existence.—R. Adcock

OCTOBER 10TH, 1903

A QUEER WAGER

To the Editor of "Country Life."

SIR,—Many years ago one man bet another that he could not move an ordinary brick tied to the end of a cord two or three miles long, I forget which. A straight and level road just outside Chichester was selected for the trial; the brick was not moved, and the man lost his bet for a large amount. It was stated by someone present that the brick, although weighing only about 7lb., would, from a distance of two or three miles, represent a dead weight of nearly a ton. I, and probably other of your readers, would be glad to have this explained.—A. W. OAKWOOD

"I, AND PROBABLY OTHER OF YOUR READERS, WOULD BE GLAD TO HAVE THIS EXPLAINED"

To the Editor of "Country Life."

SIR,—Referring to Mr. Oakwood's letter in your last week's issue, the weight of the cord must be added to the weight of the brick; this, combined with the friction of the cord against the road, is quite sufficient to account for the inability of the man to pull the brick.—R. D. S.

ARITHMETIC PUZZLE

To the Editor of "Country Life."

Sir,—Your recent correspondence about puzzling inscriptions on walls prompts me to send you this photograph of an inscription on the house of Thomas Francis, an eighteenth century stonemason, at Bebington, Cheshire.

The puzzle is a straight-forward one, based upon addition and subtraction, and should not present much difficulty to your readers, although I believe it caused quite a number of frowns in Thomas Francis's day.—Arithmetician

JUNE 6TH, 1931

CHEESE-ROLLING ON COOPER'S HILL, GLOUCESTERSHIRE

To the Editor of "Country Life."

Sir,—Large crowds assemble to witness the events. The cheeses are rolled down the precipitous slope of the hill and are pursued by the competitors. As the cheeses are apt to be smashed into fragments, artificial ones are substituted nowadays.

There are three events, the open one for men, one for girls, another for boys. Other sports follow in the interval of cheese-rolling. Many minor accidents occur during the pursuit of the cheeses. On several occasions broken limbs have been sustained.

The photograph shows the declivity down which the sport takes place. The cheese can be seen in process of descent followed by the competitors.—K. M. WILD

OCTOBER 3RD, 1908

BEEST CUSTARD

To the Editor of "Country Life."

Sir,—In the old diary of a farmer's wife there runs this interesting entry for March 10th: "My favourite cow, Primrose, got a pretty roan calf yesterday. To-morrow I will visit some of the sick folks in the village and take them a beest custard." Very rarely, in an old cookery book, there may be found a recipe for "Beest Custard," a title very bewildering to the uninitiated who do not know that the first few milkings from a newly calved cow are called "beestings," or beest milk, in the north. The third milking was very much prized for making beest custards: its increased casein content – for the nutrition of the young calf – causing the milk to set into a firm rich custard on being cooked. Presents of beest milk were, therefore, considered a very acceptable gift from the farmhouse, and many housewives liked the fourth and fifth milkings for making superior white bread or teacakes. Milk of a nature easily assimilated by a newly born calf was assumed to be very digestible and nutritious for invalids, hence the thoughtful regard for sick folks as evidenced in the diary of the

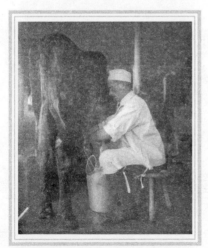

farmer's wife. Here is an old recipe for beest custard such as figured on the menu in our young days: "Heat a pint of beest milk with two bay leaves until boiling hot. Mix one spoonful of flour with cold cream and pour over it the hot milk, gradually. Stir well and sweeten to taste. Put mixture into a baking dish and strew with grated nutmeg or cinnamon and bake in a slow oven. This pudding may be cooked in a dish lined with good short pastry."—S. S.

JANUARY 9ᵀᴴ, 1948

INTERSECTING RAINBOWS

To the Editor of "Country Life."

Sir,—While sailing in the Johore Strait just before sunset recently, I saw an unusual rainbow effect. A complete rainbow was visible from horizon to horizon, with the start of an equally brilliant second rainbow at its left end, as shown in the accompanying sketch. The fragment was visible for about ten minutes and then disappeared.

I should be interested to hear an explanation of this phenomenon.— Charles Keys (Captain, R.N.), South East Asia Secretarial, General Post Office, Singapore.

[The phenomenon depends for its production on the existence of two sources of parallel rays of light. These are provided normally by the sun itself and its image reflected from a large expanse of water behind the observer. Intersecting bows are caused by the rays proceeding, optically speaking, from the image of the sun below the surface of the water.—Ed]

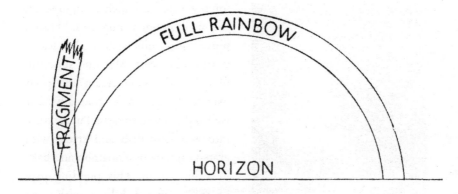

MARCH 7TH, 1903

ERECTING A SUNDIAL

For readers confronted by unusual or technical questions connected with gardens and houses, Country Life *has been an obvious place to enquire for the answers. Editors have risen admirably to the challenge. Even in the internet age it would be hard to find such a succinct response to one correspondent who was uncertain as to how they should erect a sundial.*

IN CASE OF an ordinary horizontal sundial, use a spirit level to get the surface strictly horizontal. The style (i.e., the rod or plate that throws the shadow) should be at such a slope that when in position it should lie parallel with the earth's axis. In other words, referring to the adjoining diagram (1), let the angle contained by the style and the dial plate A B C contain the same number of degrees as the latitude of the place. To put it roughly, in latitude 45deg. the angle would be like that of A B C in the first diagram. In latitude 60deg. it would be as in the second diagram. (N.B. – Inaccuracy of the slope and of the angle would not affect the correctness of the reading at noon.)

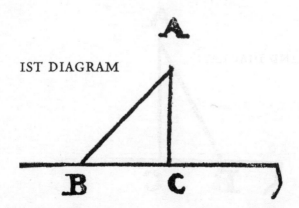

IST DIAGRAM

(2) Set the dial so that the plane of the style plate lies north and south. In the absence of a sextant, there are various ways of finding north and south. One is by the Pole star, but that swings slightly to the east and west of true north. Another is by taking the sun's direction at noon (local time), which, of course gives the south. A sundial gives the local time. To reckon the Greenwich time, for every quarter of a degree west longitude add one minute to the time given on the dial, and allow also for the clock being fast or slow according to the reckoning for the day given in any almanack. The reverse operation has of course to be done if the place is east of Greenwich. (N.B. – Four times in the year, April 16th, June 16th, September 16th, and December 16th, the sun and the clock synchronise at Greenwich.) To find local time from your watch, presuming that it is right by Greenwich time, you must allow for the longitude and for the clock being fast or slow as explained above. Thus at a place 4deg. west on April 16th it would be local noon at 12.16 Greenwich time; but on May 16th, when the sun is 3min. 49sec. – say, 4min. – in advance of the clock it would be local noon at 12.12 Greenwich time.—Ed

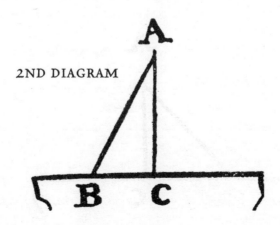

2ND DIAGRAM

FEBRUARY 4TH, 1939

A VANISHING SIGN-LANGUAGE

To the Editor of "Country Life."

Sir,—Among what may be called the more "human elements" of the countryside, that are rapidly passing away, are the signs and symbols which once constituted, and in some measure still constitute, the tramp's sign-language.

Before the days of the dole, the distribution of bread-tickets, and the free doss-houses the roadside tramp was viewed with great suspicion by police and public alike; and even if he sought the asylum of the casual ward he was there set to do tasks specially selected to discourage him from paying it a second visit.

Being thus cut off by a barrier of mistrust from intercourse with their more fortunate fellow-creatures, the old tramps, in sheer self-defence, were almost forced to aid and assist each other within the limited means at their disposal.

"WHEREBY ANY MEMBER OF THE 'WEARY WILLIE' FRATERNITY COULD LEARN WHAT FATE WAS LIKELY TO BE IN STORE FOR HIM"

One of the more interesting, and certainly the most pathetic, of the forms which this co-operation took was in the silent, but none the less powerful, medium of a code of signs or signals, whereby any member of the "Weary Willie" fraternity could learn what fate was likely to be in store for him when passing through country towns and villages.

To the regular tramp visiting a new tract of country for the first time, the signs were invaluable, enabling him to tell at a glance what his roadside luck was likely to be, and whether it would result in food, work, or the local jail. The old signs, as the present writer remembers them on many barn doors, brick walls, and wooden fences, were usually made with chalk begged from passing school children; and if chalk was not available, roadside clay was often used. As one would expect, the signs could be drawn by the most unskilled hand; yet what a mine of valuable information they conveyed!

These "pictograms" convey their meaning with sufficient clearness to need no further comment. It is, however, relevant to point out that a circle, or nought, is the basis of three signs, and means "No good," unless qualified by a cross, which changes the negation to an affirmative in two instances. The V in the "Pitch a yarn" sign may possibly be derived from the affirmative X.—SIDNEY HEATH

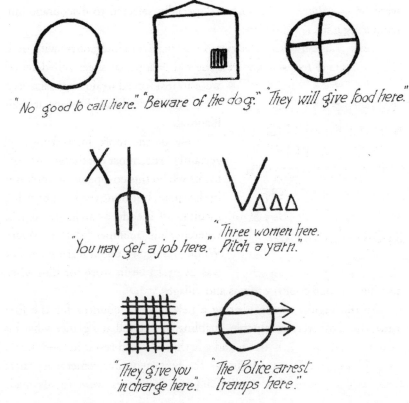

"No good to call here." "Beware of the dog." "They will give food here."

"You may get a job here." "Three women here. Pitch a yarn."

"They give you in charge here." "The Police arrest tramps here."

NOVEMBER 25TH, 1939

SANTA CLAUS IN THE BLACK-OUT

"WE'VE GOT TO be prepared!" For months the slogan shouted at us from hoardings, from shop-fronts, from motorcars, from anything, in fact, to which a bill would stick. Zero hour came and went, and we may claim, with some pride, considering our reputation in such matters, that, on the whole, prepared we were.

Christmas is coming and, as usual, it finds us unprepared. I do not believe that anybody, or at least any really human person, has ever been really prepared for Christmas. No, it is Santa Claus who is stealing a march on us. We might, if ever we had been ready for him, have found excuses without end for our dilemma this year; but no, we have simply been true to ourselves, our reputation, and our past. And now Christmas is just round the corner, and here are we wondering what in the world we are going to do about it.

"WHAT ARE SEARCHLIGHTS TO A COACHMAN OF THE CLOUDS"

Most of us may be wondering, not what we are going to do about Christmas, but what is Santa Claus going to do. Even in his experience there has surely never been a Christmas such as this promises to be.

For the first time he will sally forth in a black-out. The first question we must ask ourselves is whether he will wear a gas-mask. If "yes," will he wear his beard inside it? But perhaps he is immune from the effects of the intangible weapons with which men have elected to torment each other. Yet even so there remain the other urgent, if less grim, aspects of the black-out – though in truth we might think that a black-out can mean little to one whose age-old habitual channel of passage is a chimney.—
RONALD CART

JUNE 12TH, 1942

TENTS FOR DUCKS

The ability of Country Life *readers to conjure up cheerful associations from the least promising subjects can be astonishing. To one war-time reader the German occupation of France and the establishment of a collaborationist government there were the unlikely encouragement for this recollection.*

To the Editor of "Country Life."

Sir,—As Vichy is so much in the news just now I am reminded of the time I spent there in September, 1939, and of an exceedingly hot day at Bordeaux when I took the enclosed photograph. The tiny objects in it are small (with one larger in the centre) individual tents, red and white striped, and are intended to shelter ducks from the fierce rays of the sun. I saw one availing itself of the protection, and another can be seen on the water's edge.

The tents were set on an island in the lake which was also tenanted by a great many enormous and very tame carp.—C. L. A. Kean

JANUARY 16TH, 1948

THE RAILWAY BUN

The pages of Country Life *occasionally throw into relief everyday concerns that – alas – never change. Although the railways have now passed out of public ownership, this complaint has a familiar ring to it.*

THE TRAVELLER SEES no noticeable difference in the railways since he became a part owner of them as a member of the nation; nor is it likely that he will do so for a long time to come. As far as the trains are concerned, he remains placid to the verge of indifference, but there is one change which has been promised and to which he looks forward with genuine eagerness. The chairman of the British Transport Commission has undertaken that there will be a reform of the railway refreshment room; that room is to be "clean, and cheerful," and is to provide "decent food served quickly." It may be that we have been a little unkind to the refreshment room ever since Dickens made his attack on the lady behind the bar at Mugby Junction; but there is undeniably something depressing about the cup of tea, which too often slops over into the saucer, and the arid bun which emerges in a mummified condition from under its tomb of glass. We have much to be thankful for in the square meal to be had in the restaurant car, but the hasty snack in the refreshment room, with its chilly marble counters and its chillier young ladies, leaves something to be desired. Many a die-hard must feel that never again will he say a word against nationalisation if he can get a clean, cheerful, decent cup of tea, and that without constantly wondering whether he is going to miss his train.

> "THE REFRESHMENT ROOM, WITH ITS CHILLY MARBLE COUNTERS AND ITS CHILLIER YOUNG LADIES"

THE DECADENCE OF HORSE FAIRS

Over the course of the twentieth century, Country Life *charted huge changes in British rural life. One of the most striking was the relative marginalisation of horses, once a mainstay of economic activity and of the hunt.*

THERE WAS A time within the memory of many of us when a great deal of the trade in English horses was carried on at the various horse fairs in the country

It was necessary to walk warily at these events. There was once a buyer who noted a particularly fine bay horse at the fair. He was told confidentially that the horse had been rejected on account of his hocks, and – added the dealer candidly – "I am none so sure of them myself." The buyer thought he knew a curb when he saw it and could find nothing whatever the matter with what seemed to him a pair of unusually well-formed hocks. After a little chartering he bought the horse and sent him to his own stable. Next morning a friend looked in and was taken proudly to see the new purchase, the story of which was told on the way to the stable. Directly the friend saw the horse he walked straight up to his head and looked at him. Then, coming out of the stall, he cracked his hunting-whip sharply behind the horse, which sprang forward and struck his head against the wall. The horse was stone blind, and the dealer's anxiety to draw attention to his hocks explained.

But the days of the fairs are gone by. The glory of the fairs has departed. The automobile has, to a great extent, displaced the old bay carriage-horses.

JUNE 4ᵀᴴ, 1898

FAIRY RINGS

Particularly in early numbers of the magazine, it was clearly felt that however interesting new scientific discoveries might be they needed to be dressed up in literary clothes to make them respectable. This awkward marriage of subjects, and the florid style of their prose, bestows real period charm on the resulting articles.

WHEN RAMBLING THROUGH the country fields few people can have failed to remark circles of various sizes of grass, some small, others larger, which here and there dot the green surface of the sward. The country folk generally preferred to set them down as the al fresco dancing grounds of the fairies, the chosen spots where these favourite romantic, ideal little conceptions of the mind were given to hold their nocturnal revels to ethereal music, where they gambolled, not gambled, on the turf through the night, and of course vanished in approved manner at the approach of morn. It was a matter of belief that they danced hand in hand in a ring and hence it was surmised came about the circular form of these chosen spots in the pasture land. Shakespeare was aware of this singular fact, for in alluding to these circles in more than one of his plays he makes mention of it. In *The Tempest* there occur the lines, "Ye elves by moonshine do the sour green ringlets make, whereof the ewe bites not."

"YE ELVES BY MOONSHINE DO THE SOUR GREEN RINGLETS MAKE, WHEREOF THE EWE BITES NOT"

It was reserved for the well-known scientist, Dr. Wollaston, to furnish the true explanation of fairy rings. In a set of circles he found that certain fungi grew on the outside of the circles of dark grass. This led him to suppose that progressive increase from a central point was the probable mode of progression of the rings. He thought it likely that the soil which had once contributed to the support of fungi might become so exhausted of some peculiar pabulum necessary for their production as to be rendered incapable of producing a second crop. The next year, therefore, they would only appear in a small ring surrounding the original centre of vegetation, and each succeeding year the lack of nutriment on one side would necessarily cause the new roots to extend in the opposite direction, and make the circle of fungi proceed by annual enlargement from the centre outwards. An appearance of luxuriance in the grass would follow, as the soil of the interior circle would always be enriched by the decayed roots of the fungi of the preceding year. During the growth of these fungi they so entirely absorbed all nutriment from the soil beneath that the herbage would be for a time destroyed and a ring appear bare of grass surrounding the dark ring.

It has certainly necessarily dispelled, as is the way of science, all the romance so long attaching to fairy rings; but it has substituted a perfectly legitimate wonder in the tracing of one of those mysteries of Nature, and demonstrated once more that the productions of the earth all serve a purpose and obey a hidden law.

MAY 28TH, 1948

FATAL YEW AGAIN

THE RECENT DEATH from yew-poisoning of seven beach donkeys at Bridlington recalls a story of W. H. Hudson's. A coal-hawker with a round through some Wiltshire villages owned a train of nine pack donkeys. These donkeys he used to feed by turning them at night into farmers' fields. But one evening he decided to give them a change, in the lush grass of a churchyard – where he found them the following morning all dead from yew-poisoning. It is noteworthy that several kinds of animals seem to have no sure instinct to guard them against the virulent nature of a tree which is (unlike laburnum) indigenous to this country. Scarcely a summer passes without reports of valuable cattle having broken into some wood where they fed to their own destruction, and even birds are numbered among the victims. The fitness of the slow-growing, shade-tolerant yew to make hedges for a park in London (where the leaves, persistent for some years, seem likely to suffer from the foul atmosphere) was recently in dispute, but at least there is less risk of poisoning livestock in a great city. Fortunate yew to be British-born! If *Taxus baccata* were "another of those dismal alien conifers," without any sentimental or historical attributes, its virulence might lead to bans and extirpation. But the tree which made longbows and still ranks as the hardest of softwoods (far harder than most of our hardwoods), which is a conifer though it bears no cone, which is poisonous yet loved – such a tree should surely have its place among the English eccentrics, even though it also grows abroad.

"FORTUNATE YEW TO BE BRITISH-BORN!"

26

JULY 15TH, 1899

CUCUMBER SANDWICHES

There is a popular misconception that the cucumber sandwich is a simple combination of sliced cucumber, bread and butter. Not so. Country Life reveals the startling truth about this well-loved centrepiece of the British summer tea table.

STAMP OUT SOME rounds from slices of white bread with a fluted cutter, and spread them with green butter, made according to the directions given below; have ready some thin slices of fresh cucumber which have been drained on a cloth, place a slice of cucumber on half the round, then form into sandwiches with the remainder of the prepared bread. Cover the uppermost side of the sandwiches very neatly with a layer of the green butter, and let them remain in an ice cave or refrigerator for half-an-hour, then glaze over the green butter with some cucumber aspic which is about to set, and put them into the ice cave until the jelly is firm. Make ornamentation on the top of the jelly with little diamond-shaped pieces of white of egg, setting them in place with a little liquid jelly, and keep the sandwiches in the ice cave until they are required.

For the green butter, put a small bunch composed of equal quantities of chervil, tarragon, and parsley into a saucepan, cover with cold water, add a pinch of carbonate of soda, and let the water boil up, then drain the herbs thoroughly on a cloth, and pound them in a mortar with a teaspoonful of capers, two gherkins which have been finely chopped, and the hard-boiled yolks of three eggs; when the mixture is smooth, add four ounces of fresh butter, a few drops of tarragon vinegar, a dust of cayenne and celery salt, and sufficient of Mrs. A. B. Marshall's apple green to make the mixture a pretty pale green, and pass it through a sieve.

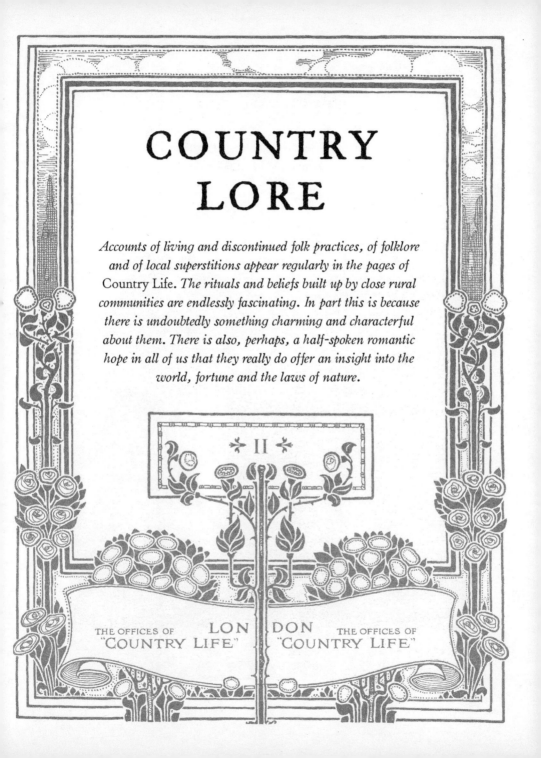

COUNTRY LORE

Accounts of living and discontinued folk practices, of folklore and of local superstitions appear regularly in the pages of Country Life. The rituals and beliefs built up by close rural communities are endlessly fascinating. In part this is because there is undoubtedly something charming and characterful about them. There is also, perhaps, a half-spoken romantic hope in all of us that they really do offer an insight into the world, fortune and the laws of nature.

✣ II ✣

THE OFFICES OF "COUNTRY LIFE"   LONDON   THE OFFICES OF "COUNTRY LIFE"

NOVEMBER 13TH, 1920

SUPERSTITIONS OF SUSSEX

*"He can't die easy. Lift him off the bed.
Maybe there's ge'ame feathers in it."*

I HEARD THE expression and wondered, but the dying man was lifted from his bed to a sofa, and I heard later that he had passed away afterwards without any trouble or pain. Seeking to know what had been referred to, I discovered there is a superstition in Sussex that if there are any feathers from game birds in pillow or bed a dying person cannot pass away, but will linger on in pain and longing.

In Sussex a few old bee gardens remain, the ancient bee-master may be met with and, although he may adapt himself to the modern methods of bee-keeping, he reverences the old customs of his forefathers and clings to the old superstitions, although rarely will he speak of these things unless he finds you really sympathetic.

It was an old Sussex bee-keeper who told me it was unlucky to sell bees, but if a price was paid it must be gold or hay. Today he estimated the value of a swarm of bees at that of a bushel of corn. If a hive swarms in May, Sussex folk turn their money for luck, but they take good care to make a noise with some tin instrument such as a kettle or frying pan to let neighbours know the bees are swarming. The swarm can then be claimed, no matter where it may be.

If the head of the house dies the bees are "told," and a piece of crepe is attached to the hive as a sign of mourning. I was told last year in Horsted Keynes that it is customary to take the key of the house to "wake" the bees when a death occurs in the family. They are then "told" and put into mourning.

"IF A PRICE WAS PAID IT MUST BE GOLD OR HAY"

The shepherds of the South Downs say that when the sheep go up to upper pastures it means fine weather, if they go down into the coombes it is a sign of rain. An old shepherd told me that when his father died a lock of sheep's wool was put in his coffin, so that at the Last Day it might be "accounted righteous" to him. This same old man told me that in his young days the shepherds of the Downs would carry the fore-foot of a mole in a little bag of sheepskin worn around the neck, to keep off cramp.

Quaint superstitions linger and are still firmly believed in; the old folk still speak of "pharisees," the Sussex name for the fairies, and at night as the wind sweeps over the Weald it is easy to credit that "there be unaccountable sing'lar happenin's down Sussex way, surelye," especially if you are a lover of old customs and a listener to quaint tales.—M. STANLEY WRENCH

JANUARY 7TH, 1939

A CORNISH SUPERSTITION

To the Editor of "Country Life."

Sir,—Possibly your readers may be interested in the enclosed photograph of a pair of "Devil Houses," which I came across while passing through the village of Veryan in South Cornwall.

There are two pairs of these picturesque little round houses, one at either end of the village, and they were built, I am told, to keep away the Devil.

In the photograph it will be noticed that they are both under the protection of a cross, and possibly their circular shape prevents his "Satanic Majesty" from lurking in some dark corner.

It would be interesting to hear from readers who have come across other quaint survivals of Cornish superstition.—R. D. Evans

FEBRUARY 11TH, 1939

To the Editor of "Country Life."

Sir,—As your correspondent, R. D. Evans, remarks, superstitions are rife in Cornwall. The curious story is told of the pair of little earthenware horsemen which are erected on the roof of a bank in Duke Street, Padstow.

They are known as "The Midnight Revellers," owing to their queer habit of descending from their roof-top perch at midnight to gallop wildly through the streets of the town, thereby scaring away the evil eye, or so Cornish legend avers.

Actually this is one of several in the Duchy, which were erected during the seventeenth century as a guide to travellers that accommodation was available at houses (or inns) so marked for both man and beast.—P. H. Lovell

JANUARY 23RD, 1932

TO MISLEAD EVIL SPIRITS

To the Editor of "Country Life."

Sir,—The enclosed drawing is of the conventional designs which I have seen executed in chalk on the slate hearths of cottages in southern Pembrokeshire ("Little England Beyond Wales" where Norsemen, Flemings, Saxons and Normans settled).

The line across the hearth and the spirals are sometimes varied and formalised trees and birds sometimes added. But the basic design remains the same.—P. V. Harris

[In his Homesteads of the Yorkshire Dales, *Mr. James Walton gives instances of a similar custom observed by Yorkshire housewives up to the early years of the present century. It was the practice to decorate the hearthstone, after it had been spotlessly scrubbed, with "a maze of pattern in white pot mould," and similar decoration was often applied to the doorstep and to the flags leading up to the door. The custom had a superstitious origin. The threshold and the hearth were places of special significance in the home and peculiarly subject to the activities of evil spirits. The intricate patterns of whorls, spirals and criss-cross lines were intended originally to baffle and confuse the malignant spirits, but in course of time became conventionalised. In remote parts of Northern Scotland cow byres were also similarly decorated and "protected." Perhaps some reader can explain the significance of the tree and the bird shown in our correspondent's drawing of the typical South Pembrokeshire decoration.—Ed]*

FEBRUARY 20TH, 1948

MAIDEN'S GARLANDS

TO THE EDITOR OF "COUNTRY LIFE."

SIR,—You may care to see the enclosed photograph of a maiden's garland that hangs near the west end of the church at Astley Abbotts, near Bridgenorth and formerly hung on the pulpit. This garland is formed of wooden hoops, bearing four shields with the initials H. P. and the date May 10, 1707, and is decorated with coloured ribbons, now much faded, and two pairs of gloves. A parchment inscription says that it was placed in the church in memory of Hannah Phillips who died on the eve of her marriage. It is said that she was drowned at the ferry across the Severn in the parish. Astley Abbotts is the only church in England dedicated to St. Calixtus.—M. W.

[The custom of hanging maiden's garlands, or virgin's crowns as they are also called, in memory of women who died as spinsters in the parish of their birth is of pre-Reformation origin. It is said still to continue at Abbots Ann, Hampshire, where there are some 40 garlands, and it would be interesting to know if it is in fact still observed. Other churches where there are maiden's garlands are at Ham, Staffordshire, Alne, Yorkshire, and South Wingfield, Derbyshire, a county that has, or had, many.—Ed]

A VILLAGE BLACKSMITH'S LORE

The rustic sage, picturesque in person as well as speech, and who overflows with information, is an eternally beguiling country type. It can never have been dull waiting to have your horse shoed by this man.

TO THE EDITOR OF "COUNTRY LIFE."

SIR,—It was from a village blacksmith in Gloucestershire that I learned of how the foreign grey squirrel ousts our native red from woodland after woodland. Well, my knowledgeable friend told me, "he guz worriting and worriting and worriting of the little red bwooy until like a stoat to a rabbit he worrits the life out of he and he gives he no peace at all. And that be the manner of his passing."

His practical knowledge of country affairs is encyclopaedic and he knows as much about horseflesh as a centaur. He once told me that the only way to make that mysterious animal, the donkey – or "buzzock" as he is often called in Gloucestershire – submissive to the human will was to give him half an ounce of tobacco to chew at the start of the journey, and half a pint of Guinness at the end. If you follow this prescription the most obdurate donkey will yield to it.

He reads the signs and prognostications of the weather just as oracularly. If, he told me, cows lying in the shade of a clump of trees on a hot summer's day rise up and walk away, it is going to be mackintosh-weather. If the leaves on the ground scamper round in puppy-like circles, the boughs whence they came bend one way and the clouds sail in the contrary direction, the skies will fall on the morrow.

His dry, sly, sedately ironical humour relishes a good tale. A sower, he told, went forth to sow, but no seed fell either upon the tilth, nor upon the wayside, nor upon stony ground, no seed at all. The farmer wondered to see such sowing of seeds, but was comforted with the remark that it would "stop they crows from a-picken of them up." This is a good example of the odd, reversed Gloucestershire logic.— H. J. MASSINGHAM

OCTOBER 25ᵀᴴ, 1924

THE GOOSE

Not only places and objects but living things can become the subjects of belief. Who would have suspected that one bird could lay claim to informing, promising and celebrating so many things?

To the Editor of "Country Life."

Sir,—From the breastbone of a goose eaten at Martinmas Eve it is possible to ascertain what the winter is likely to be. When picked, it must be held up to the light, and the white marks there discernible betoken snow, the darker ones frost and cold weather. It should also be remarked that the front part of the bone foretells the weather before Christmas, the hinder part the weather after Christmas. A legend says that St. Martin was tormented by a goose which he killed and ate. As he died from the repast, good Christians have ever since sacrificed the goose on the day of the saint. It is a popular saying that "If you eat goose on Michaelmas Day, you will never want money all the year round." It is said that Queen Elizabeth was at Tilbury dining on roast goose when news of the destruction of the Spanish Armada was brought to her, when she exclaimed, "Henceforth shall a goose commemorate this great victory."—M. E. S. W.

> "IF YOU EAT GOOSE ON MICHAELMAS DAY, YOU WILL NEVER WANT MONEY ALL THE YEAR ROUND"

BEATING THE BOUNDS

There is a strong antiquarian bent to some descriptions of rural customs in the magazine. Nevertheless, history might occasionally come to life at the hands of enthusiastic readers.

PROCESSIONS WERE POPULAR and common features of life in the Middle Ages. Many were connected with the ecclesiastical year, and among the most important were those held in spring on the three days before Ascension Day, known as the Rogation Days.

In course of time, processions came to be used for the purpose of maintaining the parish boundaries and reminding people of them. Hence the custom of Beating the Bounds as it is called, which still survives in some places. The officials hit their staves on the ground; hence the word "beating." Another form of beating went on. The churchwardens seized boys and beat them at important parts of the boundaries in the hope of impressing them with some remembrance of the exact spot.

The Sarum processional tells us the composition of the procession connected with the cathedral. It was headed by a boy with holy water, then the cross, then the lights and then the incense, in the usual English order. These were followed by a banner on which a lion was depicted, small banners with crosses, then a dragon stuck on a pole, then a shrine with relics of saints, then the ministers, followed by the choir and the dignitaries.

There were, of course, endless adaptations in country parishes which did not possess all the apparatus. In some places a picturesque usage was the carrying of what were called flower poles. These were carried at Timberscombe till shortly before the war, and they required much skill in the making and an enormous quantity of flowers. The flowers were arranged in rings of different colours, sometimes packed very tight. The head generally took the form of a cone and a big one was extremely heavy to carry.—F. C. Eeles, Secretary, Central Council for the Care of Churches

❧

MAY 21ST, 1948
To the Editor of "Country Life."

Sir,—With reference to the article in your issue of April 30th, a perambulation of the parish bounds of Hendon, Middlesex, was made by Mill Hill and Hendon Historical Society in 1946 and 1947.

The ceremony here is a revival, not a survival, for it lapsed in Victoria's day. It used to take the steward of the lord of the manor and his party two days to perambulate the "outbounds" of Hendon. Today these run, for a large part, through private gardens or populous streets. In 1946 and 1947 we chose remnants of rusticity, our ration of the Green Belt. On the way quaintly named fields were made known, among them The Round About, Witching Hill, and Farther Stockings – a name meaning the site of a wood cut down; and it was learned that the film-studio district Boreham Wood is properly Barham Wood.

Two stones shown on maps of the bounds at least two centuries ago were invisible on the march. A local newspaper account, however, elicited a report from a golfer that the stones were safe and in situ; one had been smothered in nettle, the other concealed by a tee.—A. G. Clarke

MAY 28TH, 1948

OAK APPLE DAY IN A DERBYSHIRE VILLAGE

TO THE EDITOR OF "COUNTRY LIFE."

SIR,—I think you may be interested in the enclosed extracts from a letter from Miss Florence Barber, of Marple, Cheshire, about the Oak Apple Day celebrations at Castleton, Derbyshire. Miss Barber is a member of one of the oldest Castleton families.

"The dance is always performed on Royal Oak Day, May 29, unless that day be a Sunday, in which case it is performed on the previous Saturday. The arrangements are in the hands of the church bell-ringers, who prepare the garland of flowers, collected by the children, in an outhouse

or stable or whichever public house is the headquarters for the current year. Until about 50 years ago the dance was a morris, performed by the ringers (all men) wearing heavy shoes and using sprigs of oak in place of the ornamental stick now used by the girls when dancing.

"The procession, headed by the King, who is followed by a man dressed as a woman and supposed to represent Flora MacDonald, and with the band and the dancers bringing up the rear, leaves the headquarters and proceeds to Spital Bridge on the Hope side of the village, where the parade proper commences, coming back through the village and dancing at certain definite places until the church gates are reached.

"Here a stop is made and the King, after having the top posy of the garland removed, rides up to the church tower and the whole of the garland is drawn from his shoulders by ropes up to the top of the square tower, where all the pinnacles but one have already been decorated with tree branches. The garland is attached to the undecorated pinnacle and left until it fades.

"The King rides away and the procession re-forms and proceeds to the Market Square, where the King places the posy (called the Queen) on the War Memorial and the children dance round the Maypole.

"The man who carries the garland needs to be strong and in good condition as it is a framework of lead piping covered with straw into which wild flowers are inserted until no straw can be seen. It rests on his shoulders on leather straps and covers him entirely from head to waist. A small opening is left at the top into which the Queen, a posy of garden flowers, is inserted. The horse has to be led as, of course, the King's eyes are covered."—MARGARET DEAN-SMITH, LIBRARIAN, THE ENGLISH FOLK DANCE AND SONG SOCIETY, 2, REGENT'S PARK RD., N.W.1.

OCTOBER 9TH, 1937

THE WOOD FIRE: A GUIDE TO BURNING QUALITIES

Country lore need not only be quaint. When the magazine determined to provide practical information useful to the modern countryman it could do so with encyclopaedic completeness. How did the author of this piece, for example, come by such a breathtaking variety of fuel?

THE WOOD FIRE does not always charm. It sometimes annoys because of its smoke, or alarms by reason of its dangerous sparks. It all depends upon the wood that is used, and a few notes on the burning qualities of various kinds will be helpful.

Elm, even when dry, is inclined to smoke, and, when wet, needs a good base of coal fire to burn at all. Lime, too, will smoulder badly while elder, oak, poplar and robinia all give off an acrid smoke, that from poplar being particularly bitter. Among the dangerous woods – those that spit out sparks and embers – naturally the resinous *coniferae* are the worst offenders. Larch, Scots pine and spruce, noisily crackling, throw sparks out to a great distance. Cedar crackles and snaps, but keeps its sparks within more reasonable bounds.

"ASH THAT'S GREEN IS FIRE FOR A QUEEN"

Good for heat are: apple, burning slowly and steadily, with little flame, and leaving a white ash that has a beauty of its own; crab, slow burning, with a pleasant flame; hazel, and particularly old hazel; holly – this, too, when old and seasoned – a rapid-burning wood; and cherry, slow to kindle, but an excellent wood to burn when once alight.

Ash is probably the best of all fuels for the wood fire. To begin with, it is one of the few woods that will burn as well green as dry, the truth of which is illustrated in the old saying: "Ash that's green is fire for a queen." In its burning, too, it is smooth, quiet, and clear-flamed. Beech is another heat-producing wood that will burn cheerfully green or dry. Both hornbeam and maple make very good fires, and laburnum is most economical, for it is extremely tough, and even the greenest and thickest log burns slowly and splendidly. Oak, as one would imagine, is excellent for heat, especially when old and dry, burning slowly and quietly, with small flame, but with a glow that lasts until the whole log collapses into a light ash.

For those who like a scented fire, there is a wide choice. If a really rich scent is wanted, juniper or the thick stems of old lavender bushes are excellent for the purpose, while lilac is a rival to sandalwood for the aromatic smell it gives. Most of our fruit-tree woods burn with characteristic smell, and the chief attraction of cherry as a fuel wood is its delightful scent. Apple can be termed pleasing, pear attractive, and plum delicate; and the particular value of walnut is its wonderful scent. Birch has a smell that is characteristic. Broom, too, has a scent of its own; and laburnum is very pleasant. Cedar gives off a very pleasant odour, though that from yew is rather slight. Burning larch will bring to mind incense; and nearly all the pines burn with characteristic scent. The most fragrant of all, however, is the Weymouth pine, more resinous than most, and with its cheerful blue flame this wood, more than any other, contributes greatly not only to comfort but to health.—W. A. ROBINETTE

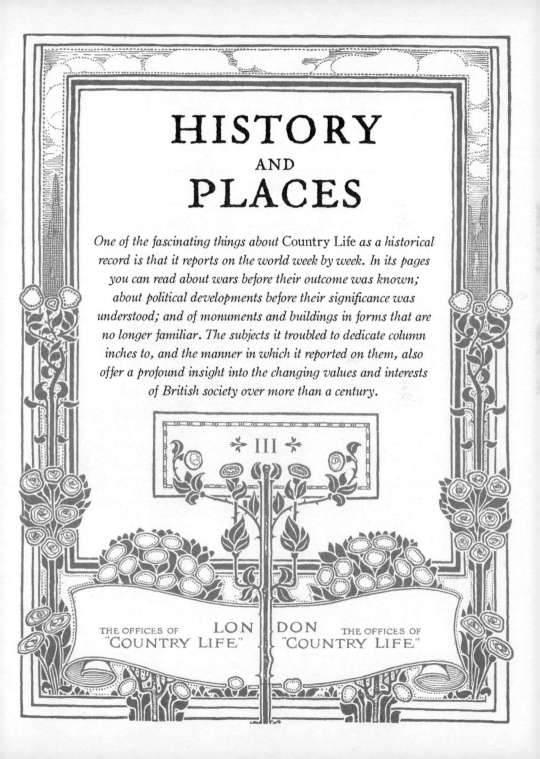

HISTORY
AND
PLACES

One of the fascinating things about Country Life as a historical record is that it reports on the world week by week. In its pages you can read about wars before their outcome was known; about political developments before their significance was understood; and of monuments and buildings in forms that are no longer familiar. The subjects it troubled to dedicate column inches to, and the manner in which it reported on them, also offer a profound insight into the changing values and interests of British society over more than a century.

✦ III ✦

THE OFFICES OF   LONDON   THE OFFICES OF
"COUNTRY LIFE"   "COUNTRY LIFE"

FEBRUARY 15TH, 1913

THE ANTARCTIC TRAGEDY

C APTAIN SCOTT'S LAST message is a document that beggars literature. It strips human life to the bone. His was a more desperate situation than ever occurred to an Aeschylus or a Shakespeare. In the wild Antarctic waste the Fates were let loose to work their will as they are not in the most appalling Greek drama. "Things have come out against us," wrote Captain Scott, and the words used so often in regard to the most trivial occurrences suddenly assume a pregnancy of meaning beside which the despair of Macbeth pales. It was iron circumstance that deepened the emphasis. He wrote them in his tent with the blizzard roaring outside and his friends dying within. Yet how homely, how tranquil, how controlled his language: "Surely misfortune could scarcely have exceeded this last blow. We arrived within eleven miles of our old One Ton Camp with fuel for one hot meal and food for two days. For four days we have been unable to leave the tent, a gale blowing about us." Tempest and starvation were sapping the last element of hope. And remember, the situation followed trials that would have exhausted the strongest. "I do not think human beings ever came through such a month as we have come through, and we should have got through in spite of the weather but for the sickening of a second companion, Captain Oates, and a shortage of fuel in our depots for which I cannot account, and finally but for the storm, which has fallen on us within eleven miles of this depot, at which we hoped to secure the final supplies."

"CAPTAIN SCOTT'S LAST MESSAGE IS A DOCUMENT THAT BEGGARS LITERATURE"

The death of Oates reads like an episode from some awful tragedy of the olden time. Captain Scott tells the story in the matter-of-fact, unexaggerated way of one who is himself confronting death with composure. "He was a brave soul. He slept through the night hoping not to wake, but he awoke in the morning. It was blowing a blizzard. Oates said: 'I am just going outside, and I may be some time.' He went out into the blizzard, and we have not seen him since. We knew that Oates was walking to his death, but though we tried to dissuade him, we knew it was the act of a brave man and an English gentleman."

Now there were three left, Captain Scott himself, Dr. E. A. Wilson and Lieutenant H. R. Bowers. There was no hope. Fate's footfall could be heard advancing, and yet Captain Scott indulged in no wild lament or upbraiding. Rather he set himself to explain how this dire catastrophe had come about. And for explanation he had to go back to the Greek idea of Fate, which is the only ultimate explanation of so much that happens to humanity. In his own words, there had been no faulty organisation, only clouds of misfortune.

Such is the explanation. We are glad to have it, because this country will, as long as it esteems valour and heroism, treasure every particle regarding the death of this little band of heroes. They died as so many of their countrymen have done before, in the midst of high adventure and in the cause of civilisation and progress and knowledge. They have passed beyond these voices where is peace.

SEPTEMBER 1ST, 1917

PHOTOGRAPHY'S PART IN THE WAR

Throughout the two World Wars Country Life *has reported and reflected on the hostilities. It rarely commented, however, on specific events or battles. This may have been for fear of the censor, or because it was felt that to do so was to place a weekly magazine in unwinnable competition with daily newspapers. As a pioneering journal in the technology of photography, however, a commentary on the use of this medium in World War I was particularly appropriate.*

THE OFFICIAL HISTORY of the war, if we ever live to behold it or have time to read it, and if it aims at anything like completeness, will be a colossal undertaking. While we await its production we ought to be treated to a series of – so to speak – side-line histories. The present writer happens to think that not the least curious of these accounts will deal with the part which photography has played in the tremendous conflict. It may sound an unpromising subject. The camera does not seem, on the face of it, to be a very lethal instrument. Nevertheless, among those who know the facts of the case, photography is regarded with no small respect; and the camera is quite seriously estimated as a factor on which not only present strategy, but the strategy of armies yet unborn, will have to count.

It records – and with a minuteness of detail, a comically unemotional impartiality which is not attainable by any Intelligence observer, however astute. Being a machine, it neither expects anything nor forgets anything. No one item in the view interests it so much that it overlooks some other item; no phenomenon pleases or displeases it, disappoints it or fits in with preconceived theories. Hence the perfection of its map-making. Here is a terra incognita whose most vital characteristics (the lines of trenches, the whereabouts of gun emplacements, ammunition dumps, hangars, reserves, roads and paths of communication, and a host of other things) may alter, so that a map a week old is obsolete. Well, we do not rely on a map a week old, when a map only an hour old – a map scarcely dry from the chemicals – is before us.

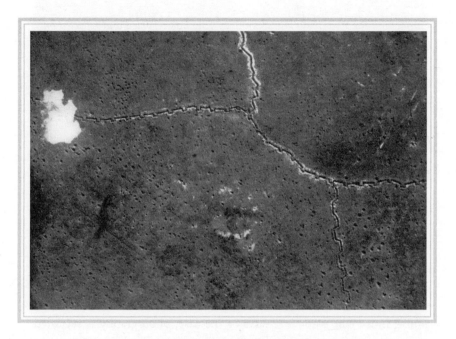

The illustration shows a heavy shell bursting over trenches full of Germans.
Note the numerous shell holes.

SEPTEMBER 21ˢᵀ, 1940

A SUNDAY WITH
THE HOME GUARD

*The magazine's own correspondents were also involved in preparations
for war and occasionally reported on them. Here a stalker goes out on
manoeuvres with the Home Guard.*

IT WAS TO be our first field practice. A lovely August Sunday
morning in this glorious corner of England. The sections met at
their respective assembly posts at 9.30 a.m. A dozen parachutists
had descended somewhere within the parish. A runner arrived from
headquarters, giving particulars. The map was laid out on the road, and
we gathered round – a very brief inspection was all that was necessary.
We know our countryside.

We had an important bridge over the railway to guard. Four of us
were told off for this purpose. We took to the fields, moving up the
headlands, and struck the railway line where it started to run through a
steepish cutting. This latter continued to our bridge a mile away. It was
like placing a line of guns. I found myself second from the bridge.

On the top of the cutting was the embankment, fifteen yards or so
wide, bounded on the outside by a ditch two and a half feet deep or so.
As I lay half propped up in the ditch with rifle at the ready, a train or
two went by below me. I reflected that this bit of railway track I was
now protecting had in the past so often carried me to such scenes, and to
many a stalk of a variety of game. Here, once again, I was at the stalking
business, one of my trusty sporting rifles under my hand. But the scene!
How different! Was it only two years ago that I sat on a hunter at the
far corner of the very wood I was now watching, and had seen a fox-cub
come out more than once and delicately nose his surroundings before
returning to the covert?

Some subconscious sense was on the alert. Quite suddenly my eyes focussed on the far corner of the covert. Something had shown for a second. There again. My heart came to my mouth with all the old thrill of the big-game hunter.

"You're a dead man!" I called out twice; the white patch had disappeared into the wood. But he came out. "Rough luck," he remarked. "I've crawled nearly two miles. Only ten minutes to cease fire and I'd nearly got through."

Two nights before London had had her first air-raid warning, and I had been in town. I reflected that COUNTRY LIFE lived up there, and that for nearly a year now she had enabled us to keep in close touch both with Nature and other parts of our lovely countryside. Hitler is not going to spoil it. It may have been, and in fact was, a first exercise. But we know our own bit of country.—H. G.

JULY 28TH, 1917

GERMAN PRISONERS
FOR TREE PLANTING

While Country Life *did take its readers to the front line during both world wars, it was much more comfortable discussing the ways in which the countryside could both contribute to and benefit from war.*

TO THE EDITOR OF "COUNTRY LIFE."

SIR,—This letter is a plea for the immediate replanting of part of our devastated British woodlands and the utilisation of trees in British nurseries now ready for planting. Forest trees will not wait a convenient season for planting. When they arrive at the required size they must either be planted out or destroyed. The latter fate has befallen millions of trees during the past three seasons and an effort should be made to save the present year's crop. In the event of the present conditions prevailing for several seasons longer, not only will our home timber supply have disappeared but the raw material for its replacement will not be forthcoming. Skilled labour for this work can be supplied by German prisoners of war. A very large proportion of the men reared in rural districts of Germany are accustomed to woodland operations, and from the prisoners in British custody enough labour could be recruited to carry out the large forestry schemes which the situation demands. One thousand men skilled in the work could in ordinary conditions plant 750,000 trees per day and would in all probability be able to dispose of all the trees now available in the private and trade nurseries in Britain. Proprietors of large estates would in many cases be glad to avail themselves of this source of labour where the reduction of estate staffs prohibits planting by their own men. That such an arrangement is practicable has been proved by an enterprising Scottish County Council which planted almost 200 acres of land in the spring of 1917 with the labour of fifty German prisoners and a few schoolboys. In this case the work done by prisoners was found entirely satisfactory and no attempt was made to evade the guard. One tenth of the men were found to be either skilled foresters or gardeners, and proved excellent workmen. By the action of this County Council approximately 700,000 trees were saved from destruction and will in time become a valuable national asset. Had this labour not been secured these 700,000 trees would have assuredly gone to make bonfires.—NURSERYMAN

SEPTEMBER 8ᵀᴴ, 1917

COLLECTION OF BLACKBERRIES FOR SOLDIERS

The peculiar interests and perspective of the magazine can occasionally help highlight wartime initiatives that have – surely – never made it to the pages of history books.

IT WAS AN excellent idea on the part of the Government to organise the collection of blackberries for the purpose of making jam for the soldiers. There is no combination they like better than blackberries and apples. Fortunately, there seems to be an extraordinarily fine crop of the latter this year, no doubt a considerable number had been blown down by the gales, but even so, an abundance will be left so that apples should be a very cheap fruit in the autumn. Blackberries, too, are making a good appearance. In various parts of the country, however, the blackberry is in the way of being curtailed as to quantity. If there is one thing the modern farmer is more determined about than another, it is the reduction of the great rambling hedge of wild rose and bramble, thorn and sloe, spreading over many square yards of land. When the farmer resolves to cultivate right up to the hedge, it is evident that he must curtail the supply of blackberries.

NOVEMBER 21ST, 1941

FIRST AID FOR BOMBED TREES

DAMAGE TO TREES by bombing may be of various types – branches and stems may be broken, whole trees may be shifted or uprooted and wounds affecting timber and bark may be made. The three agents concerned are blast, splinters and fire.

Blast may break branches, and in such cases the treatment is not difficult, as the branches may be cut back to sound wood.

A bomb falling near the base of a tree is bound to cause considerable root damage. As with branches, roots must be cut back to sound bark, and finished off with a slanting cut facing upwards. This cut must be heavily tarred or otherwise waterproofed.

Splinter damage may be of different types. If a heavy bomb bursts close to the tree, large pieces of wood are often gouged out of the butt, making a wound that can never be closed by callus growth. In such cases the only thing to do is to smooth the torn areas over, and cut away all jagged pieces likely to check the free flow of rain-water towards the ground. The whole wound must then be heavily waterproofed and the proofing must be inspected every year at least.

If a tree is examined immediately after a bombing attack accompanied by fire in the vicinity, it is quite usual to see no sign of damage. If, however, the tree is within 10 to 15 yards of a burned-out building, it is well to wait for some months before pronouncing an opinion. If leaf is on the tree at the time, the foliage will be hopelessly scorched, but that is a small matter, as scorched branches and twig ends will break again below the burned part.

Small bomb fragments striking the butt may produce types of wound, the external appearance of which differs very much. A sharp-edged fragment generally makes a cut with clean edges. A blunt-edged fragment, or one striking with a flat side, produces a rather curious wound of a type never seen on trees which have had the good fortune to escape the blitz.

If wounds are cleaned up and protected, and damaged branches cut away or braced up, the tree will probably last quite satisfactorily, until the time arrives when treatment of a more permanent type can be carried out without fear that it will be wiped out in a fraction of a second.

BARK STRIPPED BY BLAST
(*Left*) Worth treatment
(*Right*) Not worth treatment

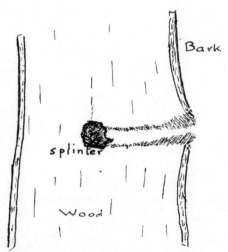

"BRUSHING" CAUSED BY A SPLINTER

SEPTEMBER 12TH, 1908

"THE OLD WHITE HORSE WANTS ZETTIN' TO RIGHTS"

For Country Life *current affairs could be a distraction from the chief enthusiasms of its editors and readers. One of these was – and remains – the maintenance and care of buildings and monuments of national importance.*

To the Editor of "Country Life."

Sir,—There are probably few travellers by the Great Western Railway to Bath and Bristol who do not look out for the White Horse as they pass Uffington Station. If they manage to see him they are disappointed, and no wonder, for he is but a shadow of his former self. Being on the hill the other day I took his measurements and compared them with those taken by Frank Buckland in 1864. The difference is astonishing. In the drawing I enclose, the white is the present horse, and the black those areas that must have become overgrown since 1864. Tom Hughes and Frank Buckland both speak of the White Horse as being dug down to a level of 2ft. below the surrounding turf. He is now level with it, and in a few years there will be no sign left of this great monument of Alfred's victory at Ashdown. The eye, which should be a small patch of grass, now covers nearly the whole head. All the other White Horses in England are well looked after, although not one of them can compare with this one in interest. Cannot something be done? Poor old horse! He is scheduled as an ancient monument by Act of Parliament; but the Act does not appear to provide for the grooming of him. A "scouring" at the present day would have to be very carefully done and the old measurements consulted. The cost of cleansing the Westbury White Horse, after a century's neglect, was £60. I appeal to you, Sir, who have done so much to stimulate love of the country and its historic associations, to give prominence to this sad neglect of one of the best-known landmarks in England.—Christopher W. Hughes

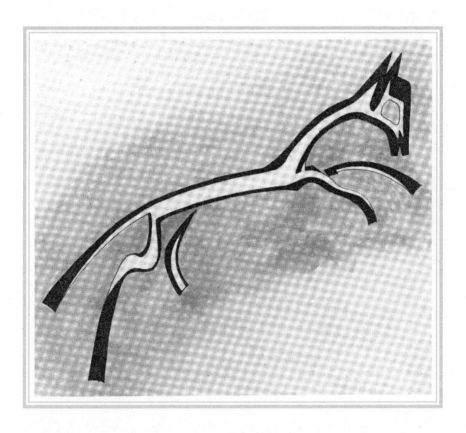

THE GIANT OF CERNE ABBAS

J UST OUTSIDE CERNE ABBAS and within full view of the grounds of the ancient Abbey stands Giant Hill, so called because of the colossal figure that has been cut out of the turf. For ages he has been a figure of mysterious origin. Who, or what, he was meant to represent remains to this day a matter of guesswork. Some will have it that he is an image of the Saxon god Heil, but that surmise does not seem to have much to confirm it. Others held him to be an effort of the Phoenicians, who, at an early date, visited Cornwall and Devon for tin. The giant is old enough to have been carved by these wanderers. At all events, he belongs to an age concerning which no written history has yet been discovered.

The Giant is now scheduled as a National monument, in sign of which an ugly railing of barbed wire separates him off from the hillside and its grazing animals. It does not shut out the human visitor as its gates are tied with a bit of twine that a knife may easily sever, and the barbed wire has not yet been invented which is capable of keeping out children. It may be mentioned incidentally that, on a recent visit paid to him by the writer, boys and girls were busily engaged in gathering mushrooms from his earth-covered limbs. At the same time they did no harm that we could perceive to the monument. In the old time he was preserved by being cleaned at an annual festival, but this usage seems to have at times been forgotten.

In the *Gentleman Magazine* for 1764 there is an article on the Giant, with his dimensions. The article is illustrated by a diagram, which is here reproduced, and we also append his measurements. It ought to be added that these were found absolutely correct, a manifest proof that the giant has, in the course of 160 years, suffered no injury from mere exposure to the weather.

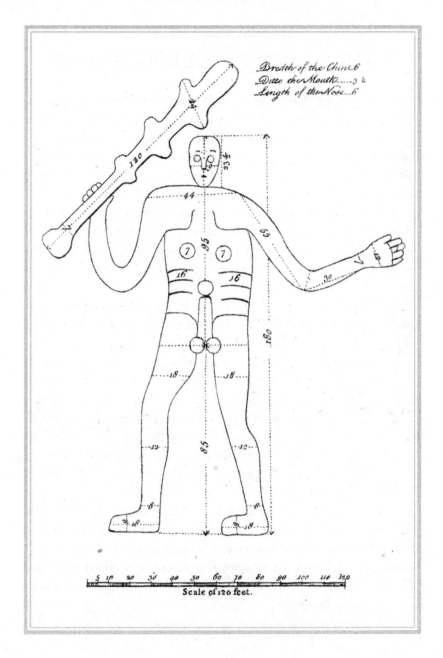

Breadth of the Chin...6
Ditto the Mouth.....3½
Length of the Nose..6

Scale of 120 feet.

NOVEMBER 20TH, 1897

DESERTED HOUSES

Country houses and their contents have of course been a central concern
of the magazine almost from its first inception. More than a decade before
Walter de la Mare penned his celebrated verse 'The Listeners' (1912),
one writer was moved to muse on the occupants of the houses that stood
abandoned in the countryside.

I T IS CURIOUS how often, especially in country districts, are to be found abodes which look deserted as well as empty; tenantless houses which display no bill "To Let," and which appear to have remained unoccupied for many a long year. There is always something melancholy-looking about an empty house, even if it be situated in a crowded and common-place street; but this appearance is intensified in the case of one of those lonely abodes which the tourist or cyclist so often passes in the course of his country rambles.

Shadows within and without fall upon the house, and upon the mind of an imaginative or susceptible intending tenant, as he with difficulty unlocks the rusty gate.

How many years must have elapsed since the encroaching ivy was trained back from the windows, or the heavy, dark branches of the trees in the garden pruned away to admit light and air to the house which they encircle.

The story whispered in the village anent the average long tenantless house usually relates to some recent tragedy. A murder, a suicide, enacted perhaps within living memory, has given the house a "bad name" and made tenants reluctant to occupy it. Some years ago a house in Hertfordshire was thus deserted, owing to the murder of an old lady by her insane daughter. Local tradition pointed to a special window at which the irresponsible murderess had stood after the commission of the crime, marking the panes with her bloodstained fingers; "and they do say that, every evening still, at the same window . . ."

It would be easy, sitting alone in a dreary-looking old-fashioned house, to conjure up the vision of that hapless little "Button-cap" who is said to haunt an eighteenth century abode in the Midlands; "Button-cap" being a child heir of Queen Anne's days, cruelly consigned to a cheap charity school, and ultimately murdered, by his wicked uncle. The victim's spirit is said to still haunt the scene of its sufferings, sometimes appearing in the garden of the old house, and beckoning to some of the children of the present occupants to play with it; and the child thus selected never long survives. There are numberless like cheerful traditions about many an old-fashioned middle-class abode.

Does the murdered little dunce of the sixteenth century still wring his hands over the blotted copy-books, which were found, some years back, under the flooring of what was once the victim's nursery? Do the ghosts of the Babes in the Wood still flit up their wicked uncle's staircase at midnight?—Lucy Hardy

DECEMBER 6ᵀᴴ, 1930

COUNTRY LIFE BELOW STAIRS

It is sometimes supposed that an interest in the life of servants is a modern phenomenon. Not so.

A T ERTHIG, IN Denbighshire, a house built in James II's short reign, there are many rooms which bear the dignified stamp of its eighteenth century owners, the long wainscoted saloon with its gilt mirrors and gessoed furniture, the little room hung with Soho tapestry, the Chinese bedroom with its green walls and tall wrought bed. But even rarer is the hall with its gallery of dead and gone servants painted in "their habit as they lived," with the implements of their craft or service. The servants' portraits, painted, it is said, for two guineas apiece, hang high up on the walls of the low-ceilinged room, and some account of each one's service and peculiarities is inscribed on a scroll.

The "black boy" is said in the *Chronicles of Erthig on the Dyke* to be of earlier date than the rest, and the rhyming dedication tells us that he "blew the horn for Master Meller" – John Meller of Erthig, who died in 1734. A reference at the close of this verse refers to William Wilberforce (1759–1833), which must date the picture after 1787, when he began his agitation against the slave trade.

Thomas Rogers, the carpenter, a moon-faced fellow, painted at his bench with his tools ready to his hand, narrowly escaped soldiering. He was taken by the press-gang, but asked permission to take leave of his master, Simon Yorke, who paid his ransom. It is pleasant to record that the picture gallery, though dwindled to a photographic group, is still carried on.—M. J.

JULY 27TH, 1940

THE LAST WOLF AND THE KNIGHT OF WRAYSHOLME

To the Editor of "Country Life."

Sir,—The killing of the escaped wolf in Oxfordshire reminds us of the slaying of England's last wolf by a bold and intrepid knight named Harrington, who resided at Wraysholme Tower, Grange-over-Sands; in consequence of this deed he assumed the wolf for his crest.

Wraysholme Tower, in spite of its five hundred years, still stands overlooking the calm of Morecambe Bay, and, in contrast with its stern purport in the past, it now serves as a shippon for cattle and storage for hay.—H. T. Morris

THE LAST BRITISH WOLF?

To the Editor of "Country Life."

Sir,—A short time ago there came to light what are believed to be the remains of the last wolf to have been killed in this country, or at any rate in Wales. Three pads have now been mounted upon a shield to form a trophy. It is obvious that they are of great age; they are much shrunken and devoid of hair, so that they may very well date back several centuries.

It is believed that wolves became extinct in this country during the reign of Elizabeth, though they lingered in Ireland for nearly a century longer. There is a local tradition that the last Welsh wolf was killed at Marros, on the coast; this may be the wolf whose pads have been preserved as we see. Another tradition claims a place called Wolf's Castle in Pembrokeshire as the last haunt of the wolf, but this is more probably a mistake, due to the name, which would seem to have been derived from some earlier connection with wolves.

In 1166 many people were killed by a mad wolf in Carmarthenshire: so there were still some left in Wales at that time. In Scotland the wolf continued to be a scourge to sheep-owners until much later: 1680 is usually given as the date for the last wolf to be killed there, by Cameron of Lochiel. A writer on sport about 1576 says that wolves were extinct in England, but that there were plenty still in Ireland, where the last order concerning their destruction was dated 1710.

Wolves are comparatively harmless animals, in spite of the legends, except in times of severe cold, or when they appear in large packs, so that a few specimens may well have lingered on in the Welsh mountains until a couple of centuries ago.—M. W.

[The wolf undoubtedly lingered much longer in remote parts of the British Isles than is commonly supposed. The late Professor Lydekker put its extermination in Ireland so late as 1766 to 1770, and gives 1743 as a possible date for Scotland. With regard to these Welsh pads, which are very interesting relics, the question that arises from an inspection of the photograph is, did they belong to one animal? These have the appearance of fore pads. If they are all three fore feet, it would mean they were mementoes of two or maybe three wolves.—Ed]

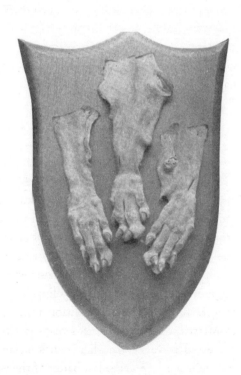

APRIL 17TH, 1920

SAVING STONEHENGE
FOR POSTERITY

Nothing survives by chance in such an intensively maintained landscape as our own. Even the seemingly eternal monument of Stonehenge, its stone circle first created about 5,000 years ago, has been actively and extensively restored. The setting too, presently the object of such controversy and debate, has been surprisingly varied in the recent past, as this article makes apparent.

As we come to Stonehenge today we are met with one of those crude contrasts between ancient and modern which always strike us with a shock, half painful, half exciting. A huge aerodrome, planted down in the solitary stretch of plain, dwarfs even the trilithons. An aeroplane, symbol of all that is new, hums over their heads, and cranes, winches and jacks are to be seen actually among the stones themselves. The great leaning stone, the surviving pillar of the great trilithon, stands upright, but other monoliths are being straightened and made safe for future ages. They are swathed in timber, as in bandages, their mighty lintel stones are being swung in the air by a crane as if they were little pebbles and then inch by inch, with infinite care, they are being moved by means of jacks back into the position they first occupied some three thousand seven hundred years ago.

The present work is on a large scale and is the result of the stones having come under the care of the Office of Works. A minute survey of the stones was first made, every stone being numbered and even the smallest crack on any one of them noted and then the scheme was evolved which is now being carried out. Questions still remain undecided. For the moment the Office of Works is anxiously considering the question of how to save the stones without doing anything to spoil or alter their looks.

I emphasise that because anyone first hearing of people "jacking up" the stones (I used an irreverent verb on purpose) is apt to rush to the conclusion that something irretrievably wicked is being done. When once, however, one has seen the work and how it is done, one has no further fears. Never was the most precious of babies more carefully wrapped up than is one of these great monoliths before the sacrilegious jack sets to work upon it. Not only is it cradled in thick baulks of timber, but every cranny is filled up and padded with felt and wedges, and the whole framework is again supported by struts and steel joists. The excavation round the base is done with the most solicitous care so as to leave intact the shape of the original holes made to hold the stones and also to salve anything that may be found there, whether it be a stone hammer, a Roman sestertium, an old clay pipe or a penny of George III. It must be a very small object indeed that will escape the sieves of those who search. How much more may be discovered none can yet say. It is another wonder and perhaps another insoluble riddle in that wonderful strip of primeval England, the land of grey wethers and barrows and earthworks.

JUNE 25TH, 1921

WISTMAN'S WOOD ON DARTMOOR

MOST PEOPLE WHO are interested in the things of nature have at least heard of this highly remarkable piece of woodland. Yet extremely few can ever have visited it; for it lies as nearly as possible in the very centre of what Devon folk call "the Moor," and in a part thereof so remote and desolate that it has never yet been fully mapped by the Ordnance Survey.

Wistman's Wood grows out of what is known locally as a "clatter" – a vast heap of huge angular masses of the characteristic Dartmoor granite, many as large as a taxi-cab, and all piled together in the wildest confusion, with numberless crevasse-like spaces between them – the whole clearly the result of the disintegration of a tor in some long-past geologic age.

Crossing the clatter and entering the wood one finds that it is an oak wood exclusively, and that it consists of no more than two or three hundred trees at the outside.

That the trees are really of very great age admits of no doubt whatever; one can infer with fair certainty that some of the larger trees are well over five hundred years old. The wood itself must be very much older than this. Local people sometimes tell the stranger that it dates from "Something B.C."; and even this is far from improbable.

That much legendary lore should have grown up around so strange a spot is natural enough. All the neighbourhood knows that anciently the wood was a sacred grove of the Druids, who gathered mistletoe from the easily reached branches of the dwarf oaks; also that pixies still dwell therein, and convicts, escaped from the great prison a few miles away, have hidden in it for short periods.

All in the district know the wood as the headquarters of the "Black Huntsman" and his pack of "Wish-hounds," whose cries may be heard on dark nights as they hunt over the Moor at unearthly speed.

JULY 10TH, 1897

A WORCESTERSHIRE BEACON

THE ACCOMPANYING ILLUSTRATION is of one of the bonfires erected throughout the country for illumination on the night of the Jubilee. The view is taken on the Worcestershire Beacon, the highest point in the county. From this spot thirteen separate counties may be seen on a clear day in favourable weather; therefore it was a very suitable spot for the erection of one of the flame fires lighted on Commemoration Night in honour of Queen Victoria's most illustrious reign.

The Beacon is celebrated as being one of the hills on which the many signal fires were lit which gave notice of the approach of the Spanish Armada in 1588. It is interesting to know the dimensions and material of this bonfire. It was composed of old broad-gauge sleepers – recently taken up from the Great Western Railway – securely clamped together, square foot intervals being allowed between each sleeper. In the crevices faggots were placed, and an iron drainpipe ran up the centre of the whole structure – which was 60ft. high – to ensure perfect draught. Round the base more faggots, brushwood, and old beams were piled up, the base extending fully 70ft. in diameter. The contents of four large tanks of oil were used for the purpose of saturating the material and ensuring the ready firing of the beacon.

Pastimes, Pleasure
and the Chase

Outdoor activities of all kinds have long been a central concern of Country Life. *As a consequence, the sports coverage of the magazine is remarkably diverse. Its mainstream embraces all types of shooting, hunting and fishing, as well as cricket, golf and tennis, but there is much more besides. In the best sports articles, the enthusiasm of the writers for their subject is palpable. It makes the people described and events themselves feel contemporary.*

IV

THE OFFICES OF "COUNTRY LIFE"   LONDON   THE OFFICES OF "COUNTRY LIFE"

APRIL 24ᵀᴴ, 1897

NEOPHYTES

ALL WHO PLAY at games or indulge in sport are neophytes at the start. Golf has many neophytes, who are both long in the tooth and bald on the head. The game has a great attraction for elderly men. With all the desire in the world, they cannot do much harm, and they generally can find opponents as proficient as themselves.

The neophyte is not a desirable fishing companion. His tackle is perpetually getting wrong; his fly goes in any direction but the right; his language is more forcible than polite; he will try one pool without success, then rush on to another; he is above all things jealous, and therefore restless he disturbs all the fish without catching any, votes the whole thing a bore, and wants to go home. Let him take the trap, and go, if possible.

It is in the hunting field and across the stubble, however, that the elderly neophyte at the game is amusing to himself and a nuisance to his neighbours. A man of middle or advanced age, having a sufficiently long purse, suddenly conceives the idea that his role is that of a country gentleman. He buys or rents a place in the country, and takes lessons in horsemanship. In process of time he finds

he is able to remain in the saddle at a faster pace than a walk. The riding master takes care of this, or he would lose half his customers. As soon as this happy period arrives he must hunt next season. Then it is that his troubles begin.

Happy for him if the day ends without his having dislocated a rival sportsman's kneecap at a crowded gateway, or had himself or horse badly kicked. He has had a hard day's work, but feels rather proud than otherwise. He has yet to endure the chaff of the dinner table, which alone prevents him thinking himself a mighty Nimrod. Chaff, whether in the manger or across the table, is most serviceable.

That the elderly neophyte is a nuisance in the hunting field there can be no doubt.—OLD BOOTS

JULY 13TH, 1929

A MEMORY OF
THE OTTERHOUNDS

THE HOUNDS MOVED faster; they were down in the grass at the water's edge, among the rushes. Viper's whimper became a squeal of frenzied excitement, and Bellman gave it deep-throated confirmation. The rest of them joined in. "This is music!" said a man beside me. "This is music!" I echoed, feeling drunk with the sound of it like all the rest of us.

"Look! Dexter's marked!" There was Dexter paused before a willow tree, poised like a pointer, one foot in the air. "Mark 'im, Dexter!" The old hound let out a great bellow, enough to wake the dead. A dark form shot into the water, like a torpedo from a ship's side. The hounds scrambled and growled and snapped angrily. Bellman was pushed into the brook, and as he turned to swim out he had a rank, choking mouthful of otter-scented water. The hunt was up.

Most of the field were in the water now, watching among the foam for a sharp brown head poked up. Hounds swam hither and thither in uncertainty. "Tally-ho!"

Sharp eyes had seen him, and hounds were holloaed to the spot, then silence again, broken only by Viper's whimpering. Dexter snapped at something dark beneath the water, and let out a fierce yell

to show he had viewed; but he missed with his strong jaws, and the dark form sank out of sight. The otter clambered out at the edge of the pool and made his way on short, hurrying legs up-stream along the water's edge. I heard the faint splash as he slipped into the water; that he should splash at all, silent creature that he was, showed that he was becoming tired.

"Forrard, forrard, forrard!" The pack flashed like lightning along the bank, heads up, mouths open. One after another they were into the stream. The otter was beaten, and far too tired to stay in the swift water of the pool.

He turned magnificently and faced his pursuers. He was splendid in that moment – his lips drawn back in a snarl, his sleek coat shining and dripping in the bright sun, his whole body poised for defence. He was alone, every man and dog was against him, and he knew it. God! I would have saved him in that moment if I could, he was so brave and pathetic and beautiful . . . but then old Dexter sprang, and little Danger, Bellman and all the rest of them hot for blood. He was for a moment the centre of a spinning, yelling maelstrom; then he was lost in the flood of hounds, and I turned away and shuddered.

Yet I knew that I should soon forget the sight of that pitiful, splendid, dripping thing; for their music makes me mad and drunk with the sound of it, and they can lead me to the river as the Pied Piper led the rats at Hamelin, the crash of the whole pack of them in unison, which is like no other sound in the whole world.—JOHN C. MOORE

JANUARY 23RD, 1909

CURLING OVER THE BORDER

FOR PURE UNDILUTED curling enjoyment, nothing can beat a "County Bonspiel" in Scotland. Especially if the county be small, so that each club knows the game and powers of their neighbouring rivals.

The draw takes place early in winter, so that the first possible opportunity shall be taken to play, for in our fickle climate ice can never be depended upon.

The day prior to the Bonspiel word goes round the county like a fiery torch; rinks are made up and discussed, stones cleaned and polished. Cold as Scotland is said to be, King Frost has a very precarious reign; the ice is criticised and weather prophets consulted, most of the country-folk being able to foretell the next twenty-four hours' weather. Then the time draws near for the start. The various rinks collect their stones and other curling impedimenta, such as "crampits" from which to deliver the shot, and by the stroke of 10 a.m. all are eagerly, nervously ready. The gun sounds, and instantly arises a babel of cries – "Soop her up!" "Give her legs!" "Brooms up!" "Never a kowe!" – all in the broad Scots Doric in which alone the game can be properly played, and into which all insensibly drift, however "Englished" be their tongue in ordinary talk.

We all meet on the ice in perfect equality, and no better instance can be afforded of that Scottish independence of character which is impatient of inferiority in those who are superior in the ordinary walks of life than the incidents that occur at curling. The laird, if he be a bad player, must, even supposing he be chosen, take his place low among the team, and his skip may be the biggest poacher on the estate; and yet the great man, if he be worth anything, will cheerfully take his place and do his best for his side, obeying orders like any menial. From start to finish the game is fought out with keenness that must be seen and experienced to be realised. The roaring boom of the stones, and the bellowing of the

78

skips giving their orders can be heard for nearly a mile off, mingled with "hurrahs" when some fine shot has raised a side to extra enthusiasm.

The Scots have been labelled a dour, unenthusiastic race, but no one who has seen a typical Bonspiel can call them that. The pent-up force which has made them the foremost colonists all the world over seems on such occasions to boil over. Everyone goes home with the consciousness that, however his bank balance may have been interfered with by reason of his neglect, this has been a red-letter day in his year.—F. KINLOCH

SEPTEMBER 18TH, 1926

ARRAN GROUSE MOORS

ARRAN IS ONE of the most beautiful islands of the West, but, whatever its beauties may be to the tourist, it possesses even more charm to those who are so fortunate as to be able to shoot grouse on its moors. It is the sportsman, quartering the moors, who gets to know and love every yard of Arran's scenery.

The Dougarie moors provide the finest scenery, and though, when shooting, one should, naturally, be more intent on the game than on the surroundings, the sheer beauty of the scene lends an even keener edge to the enjoyment. This season Dougarie moors have been energetically shot. The season has been good, birds were plentiful, and satisfactory, if not epoch-making, bags have been made. In the south of the island the Dippin moors are less hilly, but the long flat stretch of heather and the distant skylines possess a beauty all their own.

All the Arran moors are dogging rather than driving moors, and it is here, in this island, that the old-fashioned but beautiful custom of shooting birds over dogs has always been employed. The charm of shooting over dogs lies in the actual working of the dogs, and good breaking is absolutely essential, for one dog running in wild may wreck all chance of a good morning's bag. The dog training must, therefore, be most thoroughly carried out, and young dogs schooled by the example and precept of their elders.

JANUARY 15ᵀᴴ, 1938

SHOOTING AT BROCKET

ROCKET PARK WAS given its present character by a landscape
gardener of the eighteenth century in the style of "Capability"
Brown. Although it was not specially laid out for shooting, a
century and a half of use has made it a very attractive one. Considering
that it is within twenty-two miles of London and very near to other
towns, it is remarkably unspoilt.

The first stand in the morning gives the highest birds of the day. The
pheasants are driven out of a wood on top of a hill, and the guns see them
for a long way, with the result that they often prove difficult to hit. This
small wood is called Park Mead Spinney, and the birds from two other
woods, Flint Bridge Plantation and Bluebell Hill, are blanked into it
before the guns arrive. The second stand, Crackendell, is usually the most
productive of the day, and some years ago, when the King, then Duke of
York, was shooting at Brocket, 400 pheasants were killed at this stand.

The next three stands are all drives over the old racecourse, where
Lord Melbourne, father of the Prime Minister, used to entertain the Prince
Regent and his friends to annual races in the park. This racecourse is up a
valley bounded by high trees on either side, and the pheasants are driven
across from one side to the other – each stand being farther to the south
successively. After these three stands the guns go to lunch at the house.

After lunch the duck are shot. Brocket is really a naturally laid out
duck shoot, and the bridge is exactly where the lines of flight converge.
His late Majesty King George V once shot over 150 duck to his own gun
on the bridge.

HERR VON RIBBENTROP IN ACTION AT THE
LAST STAND ON THE RACECOURSE

THE HUNTING SEASON OF 1929–30

H UNTING AGAIN AT last. The opening meet is always a special occasion. We meet old friends again or there may be a new Master. There are familiar faces and new horses, and one feels that at long last the year has swung full round again. From the Shires in their unapproachable splendour right down to the little friendly provincial packs that show good sport in difficult woodland country, the opening of the season is a great event. There are town-bred sentimentalists who decry hunting, but the countryman knows better.

Hunting may be a sport for the well-to-do, but what an enormous amount of money it sets into circulation in the countryside. Not only a matter of direct contribution in the purchase of horses, corn, saddlery and farriery, but the general living and outgoings of all those people who live in the country to hunt and whose estates or houses all contribute to the workaday economics of the countryside.

Every year the older generation shake their heads and tell us that hunting is deteriorating, that things are not what they used to be. The complaint is not a new one; indeed, it is really a healthy sign. Hunting should have been killed by the car and the modern road surface, the very fact that it has not only survived, but continues to flourish, is a proof of its astounding vitality, the endless reserve of new young blood pouring into it and its natural adaptability.

The discipline of the field, that training in small courtesies and self-sacrifices which is instilled into a youngster by the older generation, is as important as skill in horsemanship or pluck in facing a laid and tied. There is, we all agree, nothing to equal fox-hunting and its charm defies all analysis. One may, perhaps, argue that it embodies in one complex thing the intense social appeals of fine horseflesh, smart clothes, speed, excitement and an element of personal danger; or one may protest that one follows for the sheer joy of the houndwork and the hunting instinct in man. But it is questionable if we need bother about this analysis of motive. The country settled it all long ago and divided people into two categories. Those who hunt and those who simply exist in the country.

ASTRIDE V. SIDE-SADDLE

As well as reporting on field sports, Country Life *has occasionally involved itself in those impassioned debates that surround them.*

MEDICINE MIGHT HAVE something to say on the question of whether women should continue to ride astride after they have stopped growing and are reaching maturity. Medical opinion on the possibility of injury resulting to the female from riding astride is used as an argument for the employment of the side-saddle; but while the employment of the side-saddle is advocated because it obviates the risks of riding astride, it is suggested that it introduces new dangers of its own. It would seem that the only way for a woman to contract out of possible physical damage from riding would be to stand up in the saddle.

The injuries that may possibly come to the female through riding astride fall definitely under the category denominated as "hush-hush," and even an indelicate medical correspondent recognises that what might be said on these matters in a scientific paper could hardly be set down here.

There is nothing in the anatomy of the female that need prevent her from acquiring as safe a seat in the saddle as any man when she is riding astride – of course, there will be spills in the hunting field among women just as there are among men, and, of course, they will occur to some riders more than to others, whatever their sex. Secondly, there seems to be no evidence that saddle injuries arising from the employment among women of the man's seat have any frequency, or any sinister influence upon the future prospects of maternity. If it was any wide experience among doctors that their female patients, if they hunted, were doomed with an abnormal frequency either to sterility or to difficulties in childbirth, such significant medical deductions would have found their way into medical literature.

My own daughter rides astride.—M. D., F.R.C.S.

MARCH 26ᵀᴴ, 1948

KNICKERBOCKERS OR TROUSERS

KNICKERBOCKERS OR PLUS fours, whichever we like to call them, have largely vanished from our golf courses. Time was when nearly all golfers wore them, that is to say all amateurs, for until Harry Vardon set the fashion, the professionals stuck resolutely to trousers. Now nearly everyone, amateur and professional, has reverted to slacks, and since they are cooler and less trouble to put on, this appears a sensible procedure. In America there seems to be a movement in favour of the discarded plus fours since someone – perhaps it is merely in the nature of a "stunt" – has promoted a tournament confined to the knicker-bockered. In this Ben Hogan, one of the leading professionals, has firmly declined to play, on the ground that he is "just not built for" the prescribed uniform. He will have the sympathy of a great many people whether on particular or general grounds; particular because their own legs and ankles are best when not too carefully outlined, general because this is still a free country, and golf, as regards its garments, is the freest of games. Moreover it is freer than it used to be, for he who played in shirt sleeves was once regarded as outside the pale of Christianity. Today the coat almost is atrophied but it is still permissible.

> "THEIR OWN LEGS AND ANKLES ARE BEST WHEN NOT TOO CAREFULLY OUTLINED"

LOST AND FOUND

With a regular golfing column for much of the early twentieth century,
even a legal judgment on picking up lost golf balls won itself a mention
in the magazine. For those unfamiliar with it, the reference to the Case of
Six Carpenters (1610) deserves explanation. The six carpenters in question
came to a tavern – The Queen's Head – and drank and paid their fare.
They then drank again and refused to pay. An attempt to have them
committed for trespass failed because their non-payment was an omission
rather than an action. The ruling was important in the development of
trespass law.

THE CASE OF the Eight Golf Balls lately decided in the High Court may not become so famous as that of the Six Carpenters, to be found in all the books, but it decided a point of some interest to golfers. It is now clear that one who wanders across a private golf course may not pick up and appropriate any lost balls that he may find there. The Lord Chief Justice laid down that "there was clearly no licence by the club to all and sundry to go on to the course and take what they could find," and the conviction of the appellant, who had been held guilty of larceny by the magistrates, was upheld accordingly. Whether this decision will have any deterrent effect on the black market in golf balls it is hard to say, but it is to be hoped.

The exact morality as to a lost ball among those who are duly licensed to go on the course – members of the club – must always be a little hard to determine. It is asking almost too much of one who finds a ball in the long grass not to put it gratefully into his pocket, and indeed is the usual course of procedure, subject, of course, to the condition that he surrenders it to the rightful owner if he can discover him. This in fact he seldom does, unless by pure chance from conversation in the club house. But recorded instances of this are rare.

FEBRUARY 6TH, 1897

BEAGLING

A PRETTIER SIGHT than a pack of real beagles spreading over a field in search of a hare is hardly to be found as a picture of animal life in any country, and certainly nowhere to such perfection as in England. The pied beauty of the little long-eared hounds, their busy and business-like action, and the keen, glancing eyes and waving sterns present a pleasing view to the beholder; while the ear is delighted with the silvery chime and merry ringing cry of their melodious tongues. Fifteen couples of these active little hunters are deploying over a ploughed field with as much earnestness as if the game sought were of nobler kind. A field of pedestrians attend them; the huntsman and whip alone being in hunting costume as far as cap and coat, whip and horn. The rest are a motley crowd, sticks, of course, in everyone's hand, as there is no fellow here but who thinks he can find and put up a hare as well or better than anyone else. Then an odd-looking old fellow in a pair of old corduroy trousers, walking straight across the furrows, not along them, as many do for the sake of easier going. He looks carefully right and left of him instead of forward; the hare being easier discerned as she lies in the furrow from the light glancing along it.

A long-drawn cry sounds clearly enough – "Sohooooo!"

The old chap in the shabby trousers has found the hare on her form. He imparts to the huntsman by a mute telegraph that he has "put her away," and the next moment the busy little sniffling hounds strike the scent, and jostle to get to the meuse through which the hare has just slipped away. Up come the panting "field" in all stages of condition, but more or less "done," showing, however, that while English sport exists English boys and English men will always be found to make their pleasure in the toils of the chase.

THE TIVERTON STAGHOUNDS

PERHAPS THE MOST popular form of all hunting in the "West Countree" is found in the pursuit of the stag. Therefore, there is nothing to be surprised at in the fact that there was a very large attendance at the opening meet of the Tiverton Staghounds – Sir John Heathcoat Amory's popular pack – at Stoodleigh Court.

They had an excellent run at the beginning of last month on the occasion of a meet at Rackenford, when they found, hunted, and killed a well-known stag who had for some seasons been known to the followers of the Hunt as "Old Bill."

This stag was fresh found above Halfpenny Bridge. Turning downwards, with the hounds at his haunches, he crossed the swollen Exe just below Duvale Barton. Hounds, however, forced him out of the water, and, running down towards the old turnpike gate, made for Higher Barn, hounds pressing closely, past Drinds Hayne, and away to Westbrook Plantations. Here Old Bill showed signs of great distress, and, turning to the right, sank into the valley to reach the river Batherum about half a mile south of Bampton.

One of the first hounds to reach him after crossing the railway line was evidently a puppy, which, in ignorance of the powers of his quarry, was approaching him boldly in the front. The stag, of course, went for him and pinned him to the ground, but, fortunately, neither of the antlers touched him. By this time the pack and the officials were all round him, and in a few minutes this magnificent stag was pulled down by the banks of the Batherum, after a gallant attempt to save his life once more, and having been before hounds for just about an hour and a half. How many times this old gentleman has beaten the hounds it is impossible to say, but, roughly speaking, I should say he was twelve years old, and carried the finest beam of antlers I have ever seen. He had brows, no bays, trays, and three on top on each side, and the largest slots by a great deal that most of those present had ever seen. The puppies were well entered, the public well supplied with tit-bits, and the hounds were called away just as the clock was striking six. Scent throughout was by no means too good, and nothing but the indomitable perseverance of the huntsman, the whips, and a few ardent local sportsmen could have brought about such a brilliant finale.

DECEMBER 30ᵀᴴ, 1899

CYCLING IN THE HIGHLANDS

TIME WAS, AND not so very long ago, when the cyclist in the Highlands was as rich and rare a sight as that often imagined but seldom realised spectacle the man in the top hat and tartan kilt. But times are changed now, and in all the roads of Scotland you may see the cyclist rolling along unashamed. The great hills seem to look down on him with wonder, as on something that does not belong to them or to their place in the universal scheme, but he does not pay any attention to the scorn of the everlasting hills. His self-satisfaction, whatever his tyres may be, is puncture-proof. His tyres have some need to be puncture-proof, for though some of the roads in the Highlands are fair enough, yet others are as evil in their surface as all are uneven in their gradient.

Passing along these roads in the Highlands, the cyclist becomes an object of the most terrible suspicion and affright to the Highland Sheep. These are active wild little fellows, with a sporting untamed look, but they are really excellent specimens of the breed, as hardy as they can be, and giving the best of mutton. But among their many virtues is not yet to be numbered that of great courage at the aspect of a cyclist. The cyclist knows only too well what a flock of sheep commonly means in the Lowlands and in England. It means a tightly packed mass of stupid fleeces that will not be at the trouble of getting out of his way, but is every moment on the point of sending out an individual to stampede across his front wheel and bring all in sorrow to the ground. In the Highlands a flock of sheep means to the cyclist white things, horned and black-faced, darting up the hillsides out of his way, wild as park deer at least; perhaps not so wild as the red deer of the hills, of which he gets a glimpse now and again on the sky-line.

A bizarre cycling experiment performed for a *Country Life* photographer.

MARCH 20TH, 1909

THE ETIQUETTE
OF SALMON FISHING

I N THE SPORTS ungoverned by written rules occasions arise, happily not often, which provoke discord and quarrels almost internecine. And of such is salmon fishing. Difficulties occur with the rods opposite. If the water is so big that it is impossible to reach the middle from either side, none of the following rules applies, except where boats are used; only, presumably, you will not fish in front of your own friends except by request.

The object of all the rules of etiquette is to minimise the friction between the enemies on opposite sides. Given a salmon pool, the first rod in the pool is entitled to fish it down first. If the person has already begun fishing, the pool is his; if he or his ghillie in his presence has laid down his rod by the water-side, and he is ready to begin fishing, it is his likewise. In either case you must wait until he has fished down a reasonable distance, and then begin behind him so as not to interfere with him. He on his part must move down a step at least, some say a yard, after each throw. If he does not do so, trouble is likely to brew. Probably the safest thing when one is getting near him is to reel up and stifle any slight resentment or pity one may feel for him. Otherwise words must be spoken. He may ask you to go in front of him. He may, as once occurred in the writer's presence, say: "You may go anywhere you like, to the Devil for all I care. I have forgotten more about fishing than you ever knew." There may have been an element of truth in this, but my friend's rejoinder was not unhappy. He said: "You seem, sir, to have forgotten something else, and that is how to behave like a gentleman." After that we went home, as, I fancy, did the sally.

MAY 19TH, 1934

CHASING THE FELL FOX

BOTH BEFORE AND since John Peel's day, fox hunting has been the favourite sport of the Lake country dalesmen. Let a pack of hounds come anywhere within hearing, and everybody downs tools and joins in the chase.

Nowadays the true hill type of fox, long-legged, grey-backed, and weighing 20lb. or more, is rare. The majority of foxes are smaller and redder, with the blood of imported ancestors in their veins. They show grand sport for all that, and still provide long runs, and despite the fact that the hunted fox can get in almost anywhere, a very fair percentage disdain to do so, and meet an honourable death in the open. The Lakes being a mountain country, hounds are hunted on foot. The modern fell huntsman wears scarlet. It is usually the only touch of colour among the field, who are clad in anything from plus fours to corduroys.

I often wish I had kept a hunting diary during the last twenty years: glorious weather in October, when the country was a perfect riot of colour; days in winter, when the fells glistened beneath their covering of snow; dark days, too, when the mist hung low, and hounds were blotted from view; wild weather, when the wind was strong enough to blow you over, and the rain and sleet cut your face like small shot. You see queer things on the fells at times. Twice have I viewed the "Spectre of the Brocken," when my shadow was magnified to huge proportions on a screen of mist, and twice have I seen a beautiful circular rainbow as I looked down upon a wall of mist below.

Fell foxes often run the tops of the stone walk, especially when snow lies on the ground. Quite recently I watched a hunted fox do this for a quarter of a mile or more. Scent was catchy, and he took his time about it. Hounds were not so very far behind him, and it was a pretty sight when they came into view. Three hounds were running on the wall top in Indian file, and the remainder were divided on each side of the wall. They hunted that fox till dark, and were heard running into the night.

LAWN TENNIS AND NATIONAL CHARACTER

NATIONAL AS WELL as individual play is one of the surest indices to national as well as individual character. In no other department of life does a nation or an individual express self so freely in public.

This is true, first, of the choice of games. Cricket is a slower and longer game than baseball. In America it appeals most to the quiet Philadelphian (the Merion Club is the Lord's of America), less to the somewhat less quiet Bostonian, still less to the hustling New Yorker. I think a people rarely chooses a game that would counteract and supplement its prominent, and perhaps objectionable, characteristics. Its games tend to bring out and exaggerate those characteristics. Both Americans and English play lawn tennis, but it is not the same game in the two countries.

> "BOTH AMERICANS AND ENGLISH PLAY LAWN TENNIS, BUT IT IS NOT THE SAME GAME IN THE TWO COUNTRIES"

In the first place, the old game, in which the opponent invariably stood at the back of the court and waited for the ball to bounce, though it is still often seen in England, has almost disappeared in America. Nearly every American makes it his chief aim to get right up to the net and volley at the first possible chance. It is not only that he is too impatient to play for safety; it is not only that his nature is to "hustle"; it is that he finds this policy usually most successful – among other reasons, it tends to put the other man off and make him lose his head.

In fact, the Americans' play is a real business, the end being success.

JULY 26TH, 1930

"THE NATIONAL GAME OF ENGLAND"

Neville Cardus combined the roles of music critic and cricket writer on the then Manchester Guardian *(and others) for fifty years.* Country Life's *appreciation of the pleasures of his prose is still shared by many a cricket lover today.*

IF EVER ANY institution was entirely English it is cricket, and no one realises this with greater zest than does Mr. Neville Cardus. When we read him we have in the very marrow of our bones not only the feeling of cricket but of England and an English summer. Even old Nyren himself could hardly make us breathe more genuinely the English airs of "that noble green" of Broad-halfpenny and of the noble ale that was drunk there. Mr. Cardus is equally at home on a southern county cricket field dozing tranquilly in the sun, with the gentle sounds of hay-making in the distance, or among the factory chimneys that look down on the grounds of his own Lancashire.

He combines two qualifications which are rare among writers on games or, indeed, on any other subject. He has the technical knowledge not merely of the watcher of many matches, but of one who was a bowler himself; he can write learnedly enough, when he has a mind to it, of the in-swinger and the two-eyed stance. He has, further, something of the vision and emotions of a poet and is not afraid of giving them a free rein. The more staid of his readers may think that it is too free, and it may be that he is now and again too lyrical and loses himself a little in his own exuberance, but he feels the excitement and romance of his game so intensely that he can make us come very near to tears, and that is a great gift.

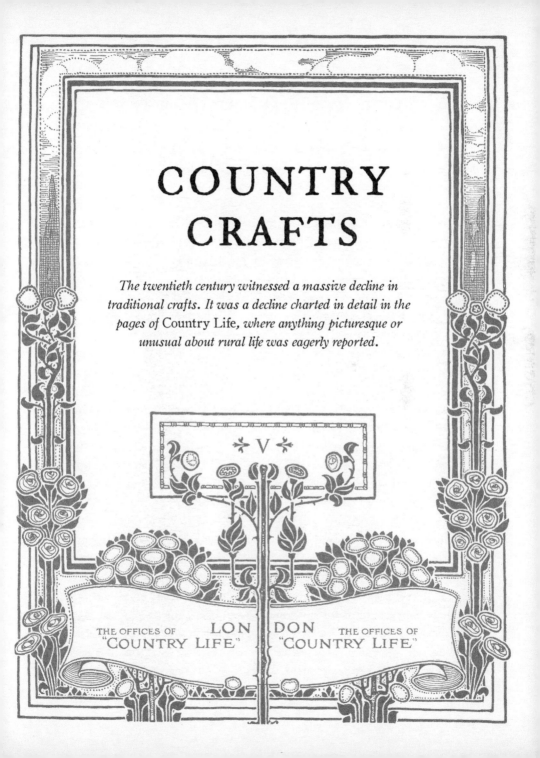

COUNTRY CRAFTS

*The twentieth century witnessed a massive decline in
traditional crafts. It was a decline charted in detail in the
pages of* Country Life, *where anything picturesque or
unusual about rural life was eagerly reported.*

❖ V ❖

THE OFFICES OF LONDON THE OFFICES OF
"COUNTRY LIFE" "COUNTRY LIFE"

JUNE 14TH, 1939

A WHEELWRIGHT BY THE WYE

A FEW DAYS ago I travelled down the Wye Valley through a village which had been famous for its shoeing smithy from 1282 to the present day. In 1282 Madoc Goch was supposed to have shod, at this smithy, Prince Llewelyn's horse with shoes reversed, in order to deceive the English army, hot on his track, as to the direction in which he was travelling.

I was soon in conversation with the village smith, who at once began a doleful tale about the decline of his trade. My informant had descended from a family of shoeing-smiths who had resided in the Wye Valley for more than two hundred years, and had made a good living out of the trade, especially at the time when shoeing-smiths were in great demand for shoeing cattle on their route through the Wye Valley to the English markets. In his boyhood days, he remarked, people would have thought it quite impossible for farmers to carry on without the village blacksmith, but all the work he now had was a day every fortnight at the wheelwright's a few miles down the valley, preparing and fitting iron tyres on wooden wheels for the farmers' carts.

Describing how this work was done, he said that, when all was ready, the iron bands were placed on the peat or turf fire in accordance with the method practised in that district from time immemorial, and then the day's work began in earnest, with little respite till the allotted work for the day was completed.

Inspired by this conversation, and eager to see what was going on in the district of Erwood, I visited Mr. Fred Jones' wheelwright's shop, where I found three men busy at work.

Mr. Fred Jones is hopeful that the wheelwright industry has passed through its worst time, for it is found that rubber tyres are not suitable for those side-land farms where the ground is soft and slippery. Welsh farmers, he said, are conservative by nature, and what suited their forefathers is good enough for them.—ROGER WILLIAMS

JULY 28ᵀᴴ, 1944

BARGE PAINTING:
A TRADITIONAL ART

EVERY SCHOOLBOY KNOWS that England was once more full of colour, in both a literal and metaphoric sense, than it is now. Houses were once as gay as Italian villas; ships, boats, carts and even tombstones were brightly painted.

It is an ancient custom to paint an eye on a boat, either as a charm, or to endow it with life. I have noticed barges of the Thames Steam Tug and Lighterage Company, with their trademark, a lined diamond, painted twice on the stern, which, together with the nose-like tiller, gives them an uncanny anthropomorphic appearance. The bargees are well known for their love of colour and gaudy pattern, which is understandable since many of them are of gypsy extraction.

I have interviewed recently men who paint barges at the depots on the Grand Union Canal. Of these, Mr. Frank Jones is a craftsman of some reputation, having shown painted tin-ware at Heal's, and in the English Arts and Crafts show now touring America. Barge hulls are usually black, and colour is applied to the tiller, fore-end, cabin, the tarpaulin-stands, and the cabin-block supporting the gang-planks. There are two elements in the design: landscape panels, and sprigs of roses and daisies.

As for origins, the painters themselves are ignorant. One bargee told me that they "liked the flowers – and it all went back 100 years ago." An old carpenter explained that the bargees owned much of the Staffordshire pottery, "big old teapots with the roses and castles." Thus this craft is a real folk-craft – unconscious of its origins, but still persistent in tradition.

Barge, the Albert, Grand Union Canal, Aylesbury. Colours: ultramarine, pink, green, black, white, crimson

Linslade wharf.

OCTOBER 23RD, 1926

THE BOWL-MAKER

To the Editor of "Country Life."

Sir,—The county of Berkshire is famous for many rural crafts, and even now the old bowl-maker of Bucklebury proudly carries on the craft that has been handed down to him from many generations of his forebears; but he is the last of his race, his only son was killed in the Great War. Tucked away in a distant corner of a lonely common this old bowl-maker works on at his homely craft. His workshop, unapproached by modern roadway but by a winding lane gutted deep with wheel ruts, appears as a forlorn relic of a one-time flourishing trade. Patched here and there with odd slabs of wood, and even, in one place, with the remnant of an advertisement board – how ironic! – it shows but little evidence of former prosperity. The inside, rough and time-worn as the out, is equipped crudely with an old-fashioned foot-lathe that revolves a holly stick curved at one end to hold the turning knife. From this old lathe bowls of elm wood of perfect symmetry and smoothness are turned. Surely, such trade as the stores can get for this old bowl-maker is maintained by lovers of everything that is old-fashioned.—Cameron Munro

"SUCH TRADE AS THE STORES CAN GET FOR THIS OLD BOWL-MAKER IS MAINTAINED BY LOVERS OF EVERYTHING THAT IS OLD-FASHIONED"

JUNE 18ᵀᴴ, 1943

BRITAIN'S OLDEST CRAFT

OUTSIDE VARIOUS HOUSES in the village of Brandon on the borders of Norfolk and Suffolk, may be seen a notice to the effect that the oldest craft in the world may be found within. This is flint knapping, which is carried on there still in much the same way as in the Neolithic Age.

Originally the only substance available for all the needs of man in the way of weapons and tools which needed a sharp point or a cutting edge, it now has uses which are necessarily very different and limited. Indeed for a long time flint was principally needed for striking fire or a light: it is only about 100 years since the invention of matches superseded the tinder-box with its flint from which to strike the kindling spark.

Besides the homely "striker-lights" there was a steady demand, after the invention of gunpowder, for gun-flints. From 1686 to 1835, flint-lock muskets were used by the British Army. Some of these weapons are still in use among the natives of the Gold Coast and, it is said, parts of China, and their needs have been supplied from Brandon. Hence the continued manufacture there of gun-flints.

Sixty years ago there were some 50 men engaged in the industry; today there are not more than six, and it seems evident that it may die out, at any rate in its more skilled form.

The first process is quartering: considerable force is needed to hammer off the projections and still more skill to know just where to strike so as to leave the necessary square edges. The next, flaking, is the most skilled of all. When the outer flakes have all been struck off it is possible to produce with every stroke of the hammer a perfectly even flake that will cut like a knife. Lastly comes the actual knapping. Laying the flake upon a bar, he taps it into smaller pieces and rapidly finishes off the gun-flakes with a few more taps to give them a neatly finished edge. The knapping operation is done so quickly that the eye can hardly follow the movements of the hammer.

APRIL 27TH, 1901

THE OLD WOODCUTTER

THE TYPE OF artist represented by the old gentleman in the picture, hard at work with his axe, and skilfully fashioning out a rung, is one that it is increasingly difficult to find. It is, in fact, highly-skilled labour with the very simplest tools – that explains the class of work fairly enough – and it is work that is constantly being ousted from the market by the more exact and cheaper output of the machine. Although the latter supplies the general need far more quickly and abundantly than the old-time workman, there is a quality of durability about his products that we do not always find in the like things made by the machine. It is too much to say that there is the difference between them which exists between cast iron and wrought; that, no doubt, would be to overstate the case. But there is this analogy that whereas the work turned out by the individual is done with the knowledge of long experience and with intelligent selection, the work of the machine is unintelligent work. The machine will turn you out a rung with a rotten spot in it as glibly as a sound rung, an offence that a workman of the old-fashioned type – for the old-fashioned men were conscientious – would never commit; even as a piece of cast-iron may be soft or brittle, but the wrought-iron has been tried by the fire and hammer of the smith.

These men, who have used the axe all their lives, will do wonderful things with the seeming clumsy weapon, carving as neatly as an untried hand can carve with a penknife, and working the wood into form at a great pace. The complaint is constant and increasing, that the man to do odd jobs, to turn his attention to the thousand and one things, none of them singly of importance, that always require doing in the country, is very hard to find nowadays. It is a penalty that we pay for the invaluable saving of labour which we owe to machinery; but it is pleasant to find a few of the old type left.

APRIL 3ᴿᴰ, 1942

TRUG-MAKERS OF SUSSEX

WHEN THE DAY of the fruit harvest draws near the need for baskets grows. Helping to meet this need is the Sussex trug-basket industry. In a tiny hamlet in East Sussex the old craft of trug-making is still carried on.

Trugs, which are rectangular-shaped shallow wooden baskets, are made from willow and chestnut. Medium-sized trees are felled and stacked to season for a while before being split and sawn up into convenient boards according to the size of trug being made. Next these boards are shaved down with a draw-knife until they become thin pliable slats with tapered ends and sides. The slats are made from willow and are fitted inside a chestnut frame which also forms the handle.

"THE WAR IS HAVING A CRIPPLING EFFECT ON THE TRUG INDUSTRY"

To enable the chestnut strips to be bent to form the frame they are put in a steam oven for fifteen minutes. This prevents them from splitting when they are bent round an adjustable frame to be shaped.

The war is having a crippling effect on the trug industry. Most of the apprentices have been called up, and as it takes over ten years to become reasonably expert, the outlook is not promising. However, this fact has been realised by the Sussex Rural Industries Community, who are making every effort to ease the situation.

Meanwhile, the remaining craftsmen are carrying on as well as they can to provide the baskets soon to be required in thousands for the harvesting of peas, tomatoes, plums, apples and other vital foods being grown for the country's larder.—IAN N. DODD

TRADITIONAL WELSH TURNERY

THE TURNING OF wooden vessels on a lathe is certainly one of the ancient crafts that survive from prehistoric times.

In Wales, wooden bowls and spoons are still made for use in some districts and for serving the "cawl," or thick broth, of old Wales.

The woods of Glen Cych, the principal seat of this ancient industry, have always been famed for their sycamore, and this is the wood preferred for all domestic purposes. It is white and easy to work and to keep clean in use.

All these traditional crafts are hereditary and have probably been carried on in the same place for many generations. It has been found that a break of only one generation causes a great loss of skill that takes long years to recover.

Since war broke out, one of the best known Welsh turners has died, William Rees of Henllan in the Teifi Valley. He was a master craftsman indeed, and was often to be seen demonstrating the work at agricultural and rural industries shows. At one time he was teaching apprentices, but the art takes very long to learn. One of his greatest adventures, for he spoke little English, was a visit to London for an exhibition.

The traditional forms of these Welsh-turned vessels have a distinctive beauty of line and finish, with perfect fitness for their purpose; and archaeologists have discerned an unmistakable resemblance in form between them and the remains of wooden vessels found in excavating prehistoric villages both in this country and on the Continent, especially in the Swiss lake villages. The conclusion is that this craft was brought to Britain with some wave of immigration perhaps three thousand years ago, and now lingers only in these remote western valleys. Small wonder that its tradition is handed down in Wales with immense family pride: along the Teifi Valley many of the people belong to one of the oldest racial types in the country.—M. WIGHT

DECEMBER 23RD, 1899

CIDER-MAKING

THE PREPARATIONS FOR the new cider make are carried out with something of the joy inspired by the vintage in sunnier France and Italy. So far it has consisted of gathering apples. The labourers carry a bushel of apples to the mill. There is much tasting of them, in which cheerful assistance is given by the farmer's younger children. The old ciderist pronounces the fruit fit and good. He has superintended operations of the same kind for forty years, and is one of the drollest characters about the place. Doubts have been expressed as to whether in the course of that period he has ever been sober for two consecutive days, yet he has a clear eye, white teeth, and a capital digestion – all due, he says, to cider.

The mill is an old-fashioned stone one, of which the motor power is an old horse that has been so often engaged in similar work that practically it "goes of itself," though a boy is present to give it an occasional reminder. Dobbin gets the word to start; then the great stone wheel begins to revolve, and the apples, pips, rind, and all, are crushed to a pulp. Our ciderist believes in a good crushing, and will not let the pulp be removed till he knows by feeling it with his fingers that it is quite smooth. The next step is Building the Cheese; in other words, raising a heap of pulp so that the juice may be squeezed out. The "Cheese" is built up, first a layer of pulp, then a covering of reeds, then another layer, and another cover, till at last there stands before us – The Cheese Completed. In the next place we have a man coming to cut away the rough edges and remove the superfluous reeds; this is called Trimming the Cheese. The next step is to force the juice out of the pulp, or, as it is called, Pressing the Cheese. We do it by the comparatively slow process of applying weights.

Our old cider-maker is not so keen on uniformity, therefore the must is put into large strong casks to ferment, and become in a natural way good cider. Strangers who visit our farmhouse for the first time invariably declare they never tasted better cider. If they are competent to judge, the farmer will send for his cider-maker to hear its praises sung. But it does not make him vain. "My Father, he made cider for a score o' year," he says, "and I've been at the job for twice as long. It would be a stroardinar sarcumstance if folks could tell me what I didn't know. Your health, sir!" He empties the mug that has been offered, nods his head in approval, and with a "That be rare stuff it be," and a touch to his forelock as antique as his general get-up, takes his leave.

DECEMBER 24TH, 1938

MAKING CLAY PIPES

To the Editor of "Country Life."

Sir,—Broseley in Shropshire has been famous for its clay pipes for over three hundred years, and there is still a sufficient demand for them to keep one small factory busy.

During a recent visit to the town I was given the great interest and pleasure of seeing over the works, which are owned by Mr. H. S. Southorn, whose family has been in the business for more than a hundred years.

I had no idea that the manufacture of a churchwarden pipe could be so fascinating, or that it demanded such skill.

The clay, of suitable consistency, is rolled into the semblance of a pipe by Mrs. Annie Taylor, Broseley's oldest pipe-maker, who is seen in the photograph performing the next operation, boring the stem. This involves threading some twenty inches of sloppy clay on to a wire so that the latter passes down the centre of the slender column. She does this at remarkable speed, and the skill required is best appreciated by trying to do it oneself, even slowly, without letting the end of the wire break through the clay. The pipe is then placed in the mould, which is seen open in the photograph, and gripped in the vice seen on Mrs. Taylor's left. By lowering the long lever she forces the punch into the mould to form the hollow of the pipe bowl. The pipes, after trimming, are carefully packed, by the proprietor himself, into "saggars" or fire-pots, which are shaped to give the stems their characteristic curve. After firing, the mouthpieces are tipped with spirit varnish, and the pipes are ready for the market.— Edward M. Lake

JULY 28TH, 1944

DRY-STONE-WALLERS
OF THE FELLS

THE DRY-STONE walls of the Lake District, which spread like a spider's web for hundreds of miles, have for years excited the wonder of wayfarers. It required something to place them in position.

The fells used to be open land until some enterprising person "grabbed off" a portion. Most of the fell walls today date back to the enclosures that were made in the latter part of the eighteenth century. The farmers were then enclosing their commons and improving them with burning, paring, liming and so forth; by 1772 the Grasmere fells were noted as already marked everywhere by partition walls. Built very largely in the interests of sheep farmers, the walls are often being allowed to collapse – and in places the conditions are slowly going back to the old days of open commons.

An elderly Lakeland worthy, the stalwart John Newton of Ambleside, told me in his stone-mason's yard that these walls need an expert hand, for every stone has its proper "face" and there is an art in building the walls without mortar to withstand wind and rain, and to ensure that ice and snow cannot form inside.

It may be asked how the walls affect the other denizens of the Lake District, the sheep. A south-country sheep would stare with amazement at the agility with which those of the Lakes, and even the youngest of lambs, clamber over the walls. And there are gaps in them, about 500 yds. apart, through which the sheep can make their way when the snow comes. Thus they can reach the lower regions without going the full length of the wall. Alas! they are not always so clever, for they have a tendency to seek refuge under the shelter of a wall and there they may be buried under a snowdrift. Sheep have been known to remain up to 40 days in the snow and survive that ordeal. In order to protect themselves from starving they eat, as a last resource, their own wool.—HENRY BAERLEIN

MARCH 21ˢᵀ, 1952

FOR CATCHING SALMON

To the Editor of "Country Life."

Sir,—Mr. Lockley's interesting article on the making of lobster pots prompts me to send you photographs of a kype basket as used on the Severn for catching salmon. These baskets are made in three parts: the kype or mouth, the butt or waist and the voreel or forewell. These are tied together and staked out in certain parts of the river bed. Mr. Bob Knapp, well-known salmon fisherman and basket-maker of Oldbury-upon-Severn, was asked to make one recently for Gloucester Museum, as they are becoming less common, and he kindly assembled the three parts of it in order that I might take a photograph.—Christopher Stringer

JULY 18TH, 1903

A MOLE-CATCHER

To the Editor of "Country Life."

SIR,—I enclose a photograph of an old mole-catcher, a well-known character on the south-eastern part of Dartmoor. Like most of those who follow this peculiar calling, he is a picturesque old figure, and fits in perfectly with the surroundings in which he works. Notwithstanding the burden of years, he is very clever at his business, and it requires no small skill to capture the wily mole. Let anyone who doubts this try to set a trap in the most frequented moles' highway. He will probably find in the morning that the cunning "little gentleman in the black coat" has made a new run right round the trap, or has entirely deserted that particular burrow, or possibly left the whole intricate set of passages, which he has been at such trouble to construct, and gone away to build, or rather burrow, a new home for himself. The experienced trapper goes round the farm on which he is engaged, and after setting his traps is disappointed if he does not capture a mole in every third one; but sometimes he finds a cunning old fellow who baffles all his efforts, and then a different method has to be adopted. Most mole-catchers have traps of their own invention and construction, and generally jealously guard the secret of their working.—S. H. N.

"IN THE MORNING THE 'CUNNING LITTLE GENTLEMAN IN THE BLACK COAT' HAS MADE A NEW RUN RIGHT ROUND THE TRAP"

THE VILLAGE BLACKSMITH

THERE USED TO be two blacksmiths living within a quarter of a mile of one another, and though both had sons, so great was the pressure of work that each had to hire one journeyman, and sometimes two journeymen. But then how different were the farms! One was a typical old-fashioned holding, with the farmhouse almost in the yard. A brook flowed past, but was dammed just before reaching the high road, in summer the stones of the dam being green and mossy, though at times of flood water passed over with the thunder of a small cataract. A broad margin of flags lined the pond, and the farm servants had their row of red-tiled cottages on its bank. The water was stopped in order that it might supply a mill-race for turning a great wheel that drove the machinery. When the sluice-gate was opened this wheel began to revolve. When the machinery went out of order – no infrequent occurrence, since it was old and rickety – the blacksmith was called in to mend it, and was quite equal to the simple task.

If you go to that farm to-day you will find the dam pulled down and grass growing where the pond was. Scarcely a cottage, except those of the shepherd and one ploughman, is left, and the stackyard is never full, because so much of the land has been laid down to pasture. The great wheel has long been broken up for firewood, and water power is no longer employed. Instead an itinerant steam thrasher comes once in a while and knocks the work off in a day or two. For it the services of the village smith are not required. Nor is the smith any longer asked to supply scythes and sickles for the haysel and harvest – these implements are supplanted by the hay cutter and reaper. At another farm standing on a hill, water was never available, and so the motive power had to be derived from horses that made still more work for the smith, but now the horses as well as the water have been abolished for this purpose. The general adoption of finer machinery has circumscribed the work of the blacksmith.

The bicycle, too, has proved no friend to the blacksmith. It has enabled many people to dispense with pony and trap, and while horses were employed he had always plenty of shoeing to do, while every local cart or other carriage was sure to come to him sooner or later, as he was wheelwright as well as smith. These changes have not turned out well for the village blacksmith. Time was when he was busy from morning to night, and his shop, especially in winter-time, was a rendezvous for all the idlers and gossips.

MAY 18ᵀᴴ, 1951

LOCAL CAKES

W E ALL REGRET the decay of rural customs though many of them died so long ago that they are perhaps scarcely worth reviving, even if their meaning were not already forgotten or in doubt. The custom of housewives in the Stamford Bridge area who until recent times made cakes bearing the imprint of a spear in memory of the Dane who held the bridge against the forces of King Harold seems in no danger of discredit on that score. Many "customary" cakes seem more concerned with the calendar than with the exact locality and it would be interesting to know whether the "speared cakes" were baked at any time of the year or only on a particular day. The only equally simple design of obvious origin appears to be that of the hot-

"ARE SIMNEL CAKES STILL BAKED ON SIMNEL SUNDAY AND IF SO, WHERE?"

cross bun, though, even here, antiquarians remind us that the Romans marked their sacred cakes in the same way. Eccles cakes, which now, apart from rationing, may presumably be made on any day of the year, were originally part of the customary fare provided on the first Sunday in September on the occasion of Eccles Wake. Are Simnel cakes still baked on Simnel Sunday and if so, where? The B.B.C. might do worse than conduct a gentle "quiz" on the subject of rural cakes, and their place in the calendar. If so we might suggest an enquiry into the origins of Tansey cake, Tharve cake and Whirtin cake as a start.

APRIL 17TH, 1920

THE ROAD MAKER

OR A TIME we tried him as a gardener, but it was not a successful experiment. He took little interest in flowers, and was profoundly chagrined when we refused to substitute cement and rubble for the gravel of the garden paths. It would do away with "them weeds" he argued, but he did not add that it would have been the only kind of job in a garden that could afford him any professional interest.

So the cantankerous Speedwell went back to the Cotswold roads from which he had been tempted, to set out early in the morning on his antediluvian tricycle – two wheels in front and a small one behind – for some spot upon those white roads flowing with delicious undulations between wide, green margins, and to return, after an arduous day with pick and spade, to copious evening draughts of ale on the doorstep of the village shop. One seldom went a walk of any length without meeting Speedwell doggedly trundling his tricycle, or limping along the road, heaving his massive body sideways off his game leg or sullenly bent over his spade, from which he looked up with a crusty stare at the passer-by. He made roads, mended them and tended them, and he seems to stand out most vividly in recollection as in early autumn, with his sharp spade he cleared away the yearly encroachments of the grass upon the cambered side of the road and cut the drains free from soil and weeds to give the flooding rains of winter passage to the brooks that feed the Windrush.

Speedwell was not prepossessing. He might have found a congenial home among the paysans of Balzac, save that he had not the deep cunning with which they conspired to exploit the credulity and helplessness of the landowners. He may have poached in his youth, of which there is no record, but in later year his lameness and his assiduity in work put this out of the question. His face was furrowed with the harshest lines which lost themselves in a straggling, unkempt beard, and underneath thick, black eyebrows two beady eyes stared defiance at the world.

HEDGING AND DITCHING

I T IS NOTORIOUS that hedging and ditching are among the rural crafts which run considerable danger of being neglected. Increasing difficulty is found in getting young men to learn crafts such as these. More and more is it the case that we find on the farms the old thatcher, the old rick-builder, the old hedger and ditcher and even the old rat-catcher. Youths are too much intent on attaining to town life to take the interest they used to take in these pursuits. And yet there are few field tasks more important than those connected with making and keeping a hedge. How it is done makes all the difference to the appearance of the holding. There is nothing that pleases the eye of the agriculturist more than the appearance of fields which are contained within neat and well-kept hedgerows. The material advantage is obvious enough, but the achievement meant a very great deal in the way of labour. First, there was the planting, when the quick-sets were set in neat rows with a paling on either side to protect from browsing cattle; then it was recognised that cleanliness at the root was the prime essential of a good hedge. Next came the patient cutting and pruning till a thick growth was established; then, after some years, the hedge had to be plashed and practically renewed – a task demanding a neat eye and hand for its accomplishment. But if the hedges are skilfully made and kept, the ultimate saving in labour and material is very great indeed. He who is negligent of his hedgerows has either to run the risk of invasion by livestock and the crop destruction it involves, or he must pay continually for the labour of temporarily mending and stopping the gaps.

IRELAND'S FUEL

Y THE LAW of compensation, Ireland, which has not a single ton of coal in her soil, has the finest peat-beds in the British Islands. One hardly knows what would have been the fate of the Irish peasants, thrifty and idle alike, were it not for the presence of this everlasting supply of fuel, lying on the surface of the ground, and waiting only to be dug, dried, and carted or carried to the poor man's fire.

We never could understand why it should be only the poor man's fire; for the fragrant, cleanly fuel might be welcomed on the hearth of the rich. Recently a company advertised high-class peat for sale in London, to be burnt in drawing-rooms and smoking-rooms; and the well-known scent was almost for the first time recognised in the "gilded halls" of Belgravia, bringing back memories of Highland cottages and lodges by Irish salmon rivers.

There is something peculiarly home-like in the sight of the peat fire. Coal can be dug nearly the world over, except, as we have said, in the Emerald Isle, even in the tropics, where the Indian mines are famous, but peat is a product of the cold North.

Cutting peats shows work going on in one of the reservoirs of fuel. The depth of peat is 8ft., and the cutters have as yet merely shaved the top. The men do the cutting, and the girls and women wheel the peats to a distance, where they are set up in pairs like an A tent to dry.

Carting the turf is a later process. This is done when it is dry. It is then carried to headquarters and there stacked, with interstices left between the blocks for air and wind to penetrate. It is beautifully light stuff, clean and easy to handle, so that women find it a pleasant task to aid men.

The "finds" made in cutting add a certain interest to the work. The roots and stumps of trees shown on the surface are found in the peat, preserved and turned black, after thousands of years of burial. Even bodies of men who have been murdered or died on the bog have been found and recognised in the peat bog, long after death, so strongly does the vegetable extract in it act to arrest decay. There is almost nothing, from the bones of an Irish Elk, with horns 9ft. across, to golden breast-plates, or chased silver caskets holding sacred books flung into the bog to save them from the Elizabethan Protestant soldiers, which may not from time to time be found by the turf cutters.

AUGUST 4TH, 1917

THE MAKING OF POT-POURRI

by Gertrude Jekyll

THERE ARE TWO ways of making pot-pourri, namely, by the dry process and by the moist. The dry way is the easiest and quickest, but the product of the moist method is so much sweeter and more lasting that it may be worth describing in detail. The chief ingredient is half-dried Rose petals, and, roughly speaking, this should constitute a proportion by bulk of something like four-fifths of the whole. Then if the remaining fifth is still further subdivided, it may be of two-thirds Sweet Geranium and the remainder Bay leaves and Lavender.

We pick about two bushels at a time, and they are at once taken to a big, airy room, a temporarily disused studio, where a large cloth, a dust sheet or a bale wrapper, is laid out on the brick floor; on this the petals are picked off and separated. If this cannot be done at once the Roses must not be left in the basket or even be laid to wait in heaps, or they would soon heat and spoil; they must be laid out, not more than two or three roses thick, on the wrapper. Meanwhile, a store of salt mixture is held in readiness; it is half bay-salt and half common salt.

The preparation jars I had made on purpose at Doulton's Lambeth Potteries; they are of strong buff stoneware with covers of the same, of plain cylindrical shape; they stand 22in. high and have an inside diameter of 9in. Each has a loosely fitting disc of lead, weighing 14lb., with a flattish handle. Three moderate or two large handfuls of rose petals are thrown in and are rammed down with a wooden rammer made of the upper part of an old spade-handle let into a rounded wooden block; then an easy handful of the salt mixture is sprinkled over the layer, another three handfuls are thrown in, and so on as long as that batch of Rose leaves lasts; the heavy leaden disc is then lowered in to keep the mass tightly pressed down.

A very precious ingredient, the earliest prepared in the year, is Orange peel stuck with Cloves.

For the seasoning I use the following ground spices, gums, etc.: Five large packets of Atkinson's Violet Powder – this is better than using the alternative of plain Orris-root – 1lb. Cloves, 1lb. Allspice, 1lb. mixed spice, 1/2lb. Mace, 1lb. gum benzoin, 1lb. gum storax. This is all mixed together and put in a pail. There is, besides, 1lb. whole Cloves and 1lb. whole Mace. From these weights the amounts wanted for smaller quantities can be computed.

We proceed to the mixing. In the case of the rather large quantity made, it is done on a well swept place of the brick floor of the studio. The Rose leaves in the jars are now so tightly compacted that they have to be loosened by stabbing with an iron weeding fork; they come up in close, thick flakes that have to be broken up by the hand, and are then thrown upon the floor. When the jars are empty and the spices exhausted, the whole is turned over backwards and forwards on the floor with a shovel. Of this new mixture none is used till the following March or April, and it is all the better if it remains for nearly a year in the tub untouched.

THE
PASSAGE
OF THE
SEASONS

Country Life *overflows with lyrical writing about the seasons and landscape. Although the language of such descriptions can seem mannered and overblown to a modern reader, the best passages nevertheless remain rich and resonant.*

❖ VI ❖

THE OFFICES OF "COUNTRY LIFE" LONDON THE OFFICES OF "COUNTRY LIFE"

JANUARY 21ST, 1905

WHERE THE FOREST MURMURS

I**T IS WHEN** the trees are leafless, or when the last withered leaves rustle in the wintry air, creeping along the bare boughs like tremulous mice, or fluttering from the branches like the tired and starving swallows left behind in the great procession of migration, that the secret of the forest is most likely to be surprised. Mystery is always there. Silence and whispers, still glooms, sudden radiances, the passage of wind and idle airs, all these inhabit the forest at every season. But it is not in their amplitude that great woodlands reveal their secret life. In the first vernal weeks the wave of green creates a mist or shimmering veil of delicate beauty, through which the missel-thrush calls, and the loud screech of the jay is heard like a savage trumpet-cry. The woods then are full of a virginal beauty. There is intoxication in the light air. The cold azure among the beech-spaces, or where the tall elms sway in the east wind, is like the sea, exquisitely desirable, exquisitely unfamiliar, inhuman, of another world. Then follow the days when the violets creep through the

mosses at the base of great oaks, when the dust of snowbloom on the blackthorn gives way to the trailing dog-rose, when myriads of bees among the chestnut-blossoms fill the air with a continuous drowsy unrest, when the cushat calls from the heart of the fir, when beyond the green billowy roof of elm and hornbeam, of oak and beech, of sycamore and lime and tardy ash, the mysterious bells of the South fall through leagues of warm air, as the unseen cuckoo sails on the long tides of the wind. Then, in truth, is there magic in the woods.—FIONA MACLEOD

MARCH 21ST, 1931

OUR ENGLISH SPRING

THE SPRING WE know in England, that shy, unobtrusive, hardly discernible spring when we suddenly realise that the miracle has happened once more, that the sober browns and blacks of winter are being displaced by the filmiest and tenderest of golden green. In the shy recesses of the woodland violets are beginning to show, and green spikes are thrusting through last year's leaves which will soon break into a glory of golden daffodil or purple bluebell.

Can it be wondered at that our folk abroad when they think of spring at home are filled with a poignant longing to see it all again: that early vernal budding, the gradual colouring of the larches and the hedgerows, the primrose banks, the drifts of bluebells in the wood, the daisied meadows, the soaring larks and darting swallows, the shadows of the flying clouds – all these making an incomparable setting in their memories for those timeless villages with their dreaming church spires, their wallflowered cottage gardens, each with a sweetbriar hedge and "a cat on every window-ledge."

> "THE DRIFTS OF BLUEBELLS IN THE WOOD, THE DAISIED MEADOWS, THE SOARING LARKS AND DARTING SWALLOWS"

There are one or two other things that we like to reflect on at this time of the beginning of spring in England. Fox hunting, it is true, is nearly over, but there is still to come a thousand other milder joys of angling, of walking the countryside, of sailing and rowing and swimming and of games still to be played in white flannels under summer skies.— RALPH JEFFERSON

JUNE 7TH, 1924

ON MAYING IN WOODS
AND MEADOWS

O F ALL THE amusements of our forefathers, gathering mayflowers, through the vista of time, appears to have been the most beautiful and alluring. Who would not give a good slice of the very unromantic time in which we live to be present again with Queen Guinevere when she rode in the month of May with a company of Knights of the Round Table clad in green? The hawthorn or may grows with us mostly in a hedge so closely clipped that it never flowers.

There are still later scenes in which one would have liked to have taken part. One was the dance round the maypole at St. Andrew Undershaft Church on Cornhill. It is said that the maypole used was higher than the church tower. It would have been a fine experience, even, to dance round the maypole in the Strand set up in honour of the Restoration. Without any disrespect to Sir Isaac Newton, one wishes that he had not taken the maypole to Wanstead and used it as a support to his great telescope.

However, it is of very little use to cry over spilt milk or grieve about lost opportunities. There are still in this England of ours easily to be found corners where the hawthorn is allowed to grow as high as it lists to grow and where the flowers bloom as lavishly as Sir Walter Scott said they did in his time at Twizel-upon-Till.

JUNE 4TH, 1898

WEATHER-COCKS AND WEATHER WISDOM

AS THE TRAVELLER is borne along in the train, especially if traversing any old-world district, he cannot but every now and again be struck at the peculiarity and, in some instances, beauty of design of the weather-cocks which surmount many of our churches and other public buildings.

And naturally, while speaking of weather-cocks, we turn to weather wisdom. Thus, when the clouds are purple-tinted red in the west, it portends fine weather, because the air, when dry, refracts more red or heat-making rays; and as dry air is not perfectly transparent, they are again reflected in the horizon. A coppery or yellow sunset generally foretells rain; but, as an indication of wet weather approaching, nothing is more certain than a halo round the moon, which is produced by the precipitated water.

The old proverb says – "A rainbow in the morning is the shepherd's warning; A rainbow at night is the shepherd's delight." And this is very often correct, because a rainbow commonly occurs when the clouds containing or depositing the rain are opposite to the sun; now, in the evening the rainbow is in the east, and in the morning in the west; and as our heavy rains in this climate are usually brought by the westerly wind, a rainbow in the west indicates that the bad weather is on the road, by the wind, to us; whereas the rainbow in the east proves that the rain in these clouds is passing from us.

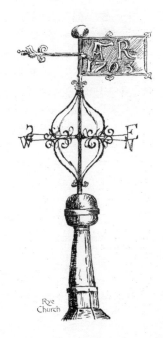

Rye Church

139

APRIL 2ND, 1910

WHEN LAMBS DO PLAY

NOW ARE THE days when the shepherd is weary-eyed and unshaven from week's end to week's end; for now his vigilance and devotion will make or mar the year's prosperity of the flock. In addition to his experience, the man's character tells – patience and kindliness, memory and heedfulness are all needed. These, as every bailiff and flock-master knows, mean the saving of many a lamb, and many a mother, too, that might without them be lost.

Shepherd Tom was moving about the yard, giving his flock their evening feed of hay, and making all snug for the night. The scene was of a peaceful beauty. From fold and sheds arose, from time to time, the deep voices of the ewes and the small, tremulous bleating of lambs, the latter in a treble of varying pitch and strength, for Tom had then been some five or six days giving these small beings a fair start in life. As I stood, leaning on the yard gate, a creamy barn-owl wavered silently over the bank of furze, and perched on the roof of the opposite shed.

Get Tom, in the intervals of his work, to talk, and you will find that, wiser than he knows, he possesses a seemingly endless store of curious experience and quaint ideas, scraps of folklore, old rustic legends and superstitions. He tells me how his forebears, who also were shepherds, were buried each with a lock of sheep's wool beside him, that he might produce it when summoned to his account, as a proof of the calling that kept him on the hills far from the village church of a Sunday.

Once more comes a welcome lull in the "baas" and small bleatings. Tom, tired out, lies down in a heap of straw in one of the small pens and incontinently falls on sleep.

JULY 14TH, 1944

FIRST HARVEST OF THE YEAR

IT SEEMS ONLY some weeks ago that the last of the lambs came, and now already shearing is well advanced. In the old days this was often done in the orchard, where there was plenty of space and the air was cool under the trees. If the weather was uncertain, the sheep were driven into a large linhay with fixed pens, where they lived sometimes with their lambs in rough weather, for shearing is essentially a fine-weather job and cannot be done if the wool is wet.

To get the animal into position for clipping requires considerable muscular strength, experience and knack, and the shearer must be something of a wrestler to handle them quickly. A fully-grown long-wool ewe weighs anything up to 160 lb. and, as it generally struggles vigorously, is very difficult to hold and manipulate.

The shearer starts on the head and works downwards, the heavy fleece slipping gradually, by its own weight, to the floor. It is a hot, tiring, sweaty business, entailing the consumption of much cider; one of the many skilled jobs which that capable, efficient workman the farm-labourer does so well.

There is the old and well-known story of the lady visitor from town who thought shearing much too cruel, although how she thought her tweed costume or her husband's underwear and socks were produced is not recorded. With skilled men slips and cuts are not frequent, but any wound is promptly dabbed with Stockholm tar, which soon heals it. There is little doubt that the sheep are as glad to be relieved of their hot superfluous clothing as is the wealthy lady, who is persuaded to doff her expensive fur coat in summer, or the returned airman, who slips out of his flying-kit so readily. In about six weeks after shearing they are dipped and thereafter await undisturbed a long spell of freedom from interference until the lambing season once more comes round.

JULY 17TH, 1920

CORNWALL IN SUMMER

ONLY ON A serene day in mid summer is there a hint of the truly genial in Cornish air. All around its shores the aliens from town have quartered themselves in hotels, boarding-houses, furnished apartments, bungalows: and this invasion, which is alleged to vulgarise the country, really renders it delightful by alleviating the rigour of its loneliness. There is a family-party mien about habitual summer visitors to Cornwall. Everybody knows everybody else – or this, at least, is the tacit assumption. Everybody is in picnic mood. Everybody takes for granted that old clothes are de rigueur and fashionableness bad form. Every cove along certain stretches of the coast is a bathing place. Very bonny some of them are. Hemmed in by colossal sculptured precipices, each tiny bay is almost as sheltered as a swimming-bath. Proud waves come rolling in from beyond the capes, and shelter themselves on the beach, to the delight of the children who paddle in the surf which swirls and rushes round their bare toes.

To look down on one of these bathing coves when the season is at its height and the sun has warmed the water is to behold one of the gayest, pleasantest sights in England – and one of the prettiest. The colouring alone is astounding: the blues and greens and marbled whites of the sea, the yellow of the sands, the butterfly scarlet of parasols, the stripes of bathing-suits, make a scheme which is violent yet harmonious. Cornwall seems naught but kindliness.

Nevertheless if you return to the same spot after nightfall its gloom is horrifying. The colour has faded – and, with the colour, the gentleness and charm have fled. The sea is grey; the sable crags make one think of suicide; in a maze of hidden caverns there are eerie rumblings and explosions as the surges enter and retreat. Even in windless weather, and at full moon, the cliffs and coves of Cornwall have an uncanny terribleness. The scenery of places like Tintagel is melodramatic by day; by night it is more than melodramatic, it is unearthly, wicked, shuddersome.

The sea and the cliffs seem to be leagued in a secret conspiracy to persuade one that Nature is not our friend but our enemy, and that, in going forth on to the cliffs after dark, we are intruding into a perilous realm where only the shades of the dead, and banshees, ghouls, kelpies and demoniacal creatures generally are tolerated. We surmise that should we venture too near the edge of the cliff an invisible hand must push us over into the witches' cauldron of foam beneath. Such is the power of the imagination, played upon by appropriate conditions. Cornwall at night is no place for the individual with sin upon his conscience.

SEPTEMBER 2ᴺᴰ, 1911

SHETLAND IN AUTUMN

WHEN SEPTEMBER COMES there is no portion of the British Islands more conducive to the enjoyment of the holiday-maker and tourist than the Orkney and Shetland Islands. Now is the time when the scent of heather on the moors and hills offers a delightful contrast to the pungent aroma of the peat "reek" that hangs over the villages. For coal is a luxury after the Pentland Firth is crossed, and is burned only in the houses of the well-to-do even in the Orcadian Islands. The days, too, stretch out far longer in these Northern islands than they do in the South, and that is a very great help to enjoyment, seeing that the ordinary August holiday-maker in the South of England begins to feel that the nights are long and difficult to pass away. For pastime and even for good company these Northern islands will hold their own. If the pilgrim chooses to wander over them in solitude, that is entirely his own affair. He does so presumably because he likes to be alone, and certainly there are many islands as thinly sprinkled with inhabitants as that of Alexander Selkirk.

Perhaps the most picturesque of the feathered creatures associated with the Shetlands is the skua, or "Bonksie," as it is called. It is often described as one of the rarest British birds; but the skua is in reality very retiring in its habits, living for periods far out at sea, and visiting only the loneliest headlands. It is most seen during the time when the gulls and terns are breeding. Towards them it is the most rapacious of pirates. When the parental gull or tern is winging its way homeward with a fish in its mouth the skua starts in pursuit, and as he is one of the swiftest of the birds of the air and his quarry in terror of its death, very soon the tit-bit is dropped. Often the skua will catch it before it reaches the sea, and fly to the rock on which it makes its meal.

DECEMBER 23RD, 1939

A WINTER MORNING

A COUNTRY POSTMAN'S ROUND
BY SIMON EVANS

SOON AFTER THE church clock struck six I opened the door of my cottage. The air was still and cold. The stars glimmered and twinkled in a clear sky. The village, less than half a mile away, was hidden beneath a heavy mist, but the steeple, leaning a little like a bent old man, all warped and grey, was just visible. Bed on such a morning is a cosy, pleasant place, but, when custom has made early rising easy, when an eighteen-mile walk across country is an everyday job, the weather is more important: it makes or mars a rural postman's day.

Outside the Post Office four or five postmen stamped their feet and clapped their mittened hands; in the dim light before the dawn they moved about like bulky shadows. Promptly at 6.15 a.m. the mail arrived. In a beam of light from the open door of the office the mail-van, as it throbbed and shivered in a cloud of mist, resembled a great red monster caught out of the surrounding gloom. Half an hour later the mail was sorted and divided among the men. I packed my bag, swung it over my shoulder, picked up my stick, and off I went once more.

> "ONLY THE HARES ARE WAKEFUL, LOOSELY LOPING ALONG THE HEDGES WITH THEIR EASY GAIT, AND BIG LOOSE EARS, AND PAD-PRINTS CROSSING SNOW"

Dawn had not yet arrived. Often, as I pass through the village on such mornings as these, I have a little sense of victory: all is quiet, doors shut, blinds drawn, chimneys smokeless. The grey roofs, mossy gable-ends and ivy-covered walls were bathed in a soft half-light. All the houses seemed waist deep in shadow. The crooked steeple of the old church seemed to be growing out of an acre or more of dark woodland. As I walked I saw that little drifts of powdery snow had gathered near garden walls, under thick holly hedges and in the deep gutters of tiled roofs.

I turned and looked back over the way I had come; the mist had almost disappeared, but the village still lay asleep. Now in the radiant night no men are stirring. The little houses sleep with shuttered panes; only the hares are wakeful, loosely loping along the hedges with their easy gait, and big loose ears, and pad-prints crossing snow.

GREAT STORMS

I T IS BAD enough, in the great gales, even for man, with a strong roof over his head, for it is seldom that the biggest gales are strong enough in temperate climates to take that off; but the discomfort that man suffers in the disastrous levelling of coverts and fine forest trees, and the blockading for a while of his carriage-ways and footways, can be but as a mere nothing in comparison to the discomfort and danger that the animals undergo, especially the creatures who "roost in the branches." It is impossible for the imagination to conceive a scene of more chaotic horror than that in which the tree-roosting birds must find themselves when such gales as we have lately suffered are raging through their homes – howling wind, crashing of great trunks and branches and snapping of innumerable small ones, and the death cries of those of their own kind whom the wind has forced helplessly against some fatal stumbling-block, or wedged between branches blown violently together. After the great storms, among the ruins of the trees, the keepers and woodmen pick up numbers of dead birds – rooks, starlings, wood pigeons – any kind that has its roosting-place among the trees, and even others who sleep in lowlier beds, but on whom the big trees have fallen so as to crush them.

It was a melancholy thing, and an unbelievable thing, had it not "jumped to the eyes," to see the devastation wrought in the East of Scotland by the historical gale of November, 1892. Whole woods, or what had been woods, were levelled; the trees, as trees, had absolutely ceased to exist, were lying pell-mell on and across each other, each having torn by the roots a great mass of the thin soil. They lay like a field of barley beaten by the wind and thunder rain. The night was most weird, suggesting that some race of Titans had been playing a game of spelicans over many acres. Such great storms as this occur, perhaps, once in two decades. The morrow of a great storm is a sad reckoning of the cost.

DECEMBER 17TH, 1904

COUNTRY IN WINTER

I T IS THE privilege of those who dwell always in Arcadia to grumble at the discomforts thereof. With their dislike of mud, their repugnance to the short days and long, gloomy evenings, their intolerance of what is dull and insipid, one cannot help feeling a certain sympathy.

Yet, in sober truth, the joy of emerging from the streets in winter to the full and kindly light that lies on covert and hillside is one scarcely to be expressed. Scientific men would have us believe that there is very little real difference between, say, the wind that blows down Piccadilly and the breeze that whistles across Snowdon. But, if that be so, imagination must play a very great part, for the delight in a winter day of escaping from smoke and houses to the clean air of the hills seems to be the result of applying a fine stimulant, that is, the air itself comes instinct with life and health. And in winter one feels this more than in summer, because, nowadays, there are few towns without a suggestion of greenery. London, for instance, has its street trees, its noble parks and beautiful gardens, where one can actually feel the touch of summer; but during the months of December, January, and February every touch of Nature appears to have fled from the streets. To escape, therefore, is a gladness unspeakable, and the discomforts are far more imaginary than real. And the landscape in winter has charms peculiarly its own. The woodlands now are all stripped and bare; but the trees, as they stand clustered together, present a soft, dark, waving outline such as cannot be traced when the foliage is thick upon them.

In most sober earnest it can be asserted that some of the effects produced by winter sunlight are as fine as the richest summer yields. We would cite as an example that of the sun descending through a veil of forest trees. So quickly does it go down in the winter months that the eye seems almost able to detect the movement, while as it drops it seems to widen with a more golden glory, till at last it would deceive anybody into thinking that it was an actual red fire on the edge of the landscape, the great tree trunks breaking up the mass till it resembles rising flames. Then, as it goes out of sight, yellow flags of cloud pass from it and diffuse themselves over the West.

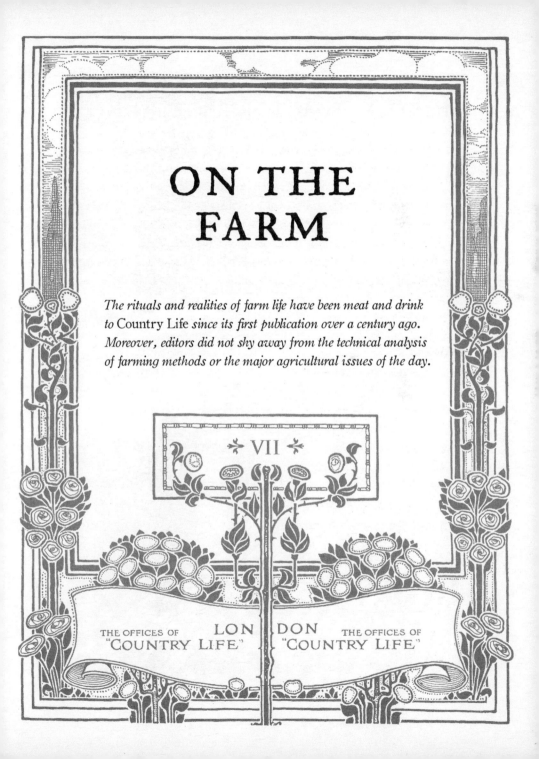

ON THE FARM

The rituals and realities of farm life have been meat and drink to Country Life *since its first publication over a century ago. Moreover, editors did not shy away from the technical analysis of farming methods or the major agricultural issues of the day.*

✳ VII ✳

THE OFFICES OF
"COUNTRY LIFE"

LONDON

THE OFFICES OF
"COUNTRY LIFE"

HORSE V. TRACTOR PLOUGHING

MR. ORWIN'S RESEARCHES into the economies of the farm have led him to a careful examination of the comparative costs of ploughing, cultivating, etc., by tractor and by horse. He has set down the results of this enquiry on a Berkshire farm for the year 1919–20. Of the 400 acres of the farm about 100 acres were under the plough, and as the soils included light sand, tenacious clay and limestone brash, the average may be taken as fairly normal, but it is the comparative and not the actual figures which are important. Broadly speaking they reveal that for the year 1919–20 there was little to choose between the Titan tractor and the Shire horse as regards the actual cost of the operations performed, and Mr. Orwin sets down the natural conclusion that "the

tractor must seek to justify itself through the indirect advantages accruing from its use. Tractor power enables the farmer to get work done very often at a time when horse power could not cope with it, even though horses are available and the work crying out to be done."

Everyone who is concerned to see the rapid development of mechanical aids to farming on sound economic lines will look forward to the results of Mr. Orwin's further researches.

APRIL 13TH, 1901

SPEED THE PLOUGH

Not all the magazine's coverage of farming was so earnest. There was
also plenty of space for describing country customs, celebrating farming
curiosities or even just describing farming life.

THE TOAST DRUNK at all the old-fashioned farmers' gatherings, and
drunk in March ale or Brown October at the spring and autumn
sowings, was that which forms the title of this article. March sees
the last ploughing for the seed-bed of spring corn. March winds get the
soil ready, crumbling all the ridges of the winter furrows, which frost
and rain have already done their best to loosen and break up. Spring
ploughing is a far more cheerful business, and lighter work than that of
autumn and winter.

JULY 9TH, 1943

THE "COUNTRY LIFE" ESTATE

A THOUSAND ACRES IN BERKSHIRE AND
WHAT WE PROPOSE TO DO WITH IT

It is a mark of just how seriously the magazine took its coverage of farming that during the war it bought an experimental farm. Reports from it were to appear regularly in the magazine for the next decade or more.

LAST OCTOBER WE stated our intention of acquiring a small estate as a contribution towards the maintenance of a progressive Agriculture after the war. Our aim would be to conduct such an estate in accordance with the best modern practice. We now have pleasure in announcing that we have bought our estate, and we give below some further details of our plans. For their full realisation we must wait until the end of the war. GOODINGS lies in a fold of the Berkshire Downs; it is high, windy, bracing country, with big coloured fields laid as neatly as carpets on the opposite hillside. In the old days it was all sheep and wheat in these parts. Today the sheep have given place to dairy herds, but the wheat – acres upon acres of it – looks a grand sight in these midsummer days, as its thick green pile begins to show the first tinge of harvest-gold.

Wheat is naturally this year's main crop, and it promises well, but the programme includes also oats, barley, linseed, kale, dredge, lucerne, and a few acres of roots and beans. The beans have more than justified themselves. We view it as a long-term experiment. The war will naturally retard our programme; we shall have to build extensively, and collect and train skilled staff, buy much new equipment and lay the foundations of sound strains of livestock. We realise that the task will not be easy, but we are not daunted by it.

Our object is to make it a link between theory and practice. We hope to convince the farmer that once a new development has received the hallmark of Goodings it is ready for general circulation.—ED

MAY 1ST, 1909

SPRING ON THE FARM

MY EYE CAUGHT sight of two figures engaged in setting potatoes in a field perhaps a hundred and fifty yards away. They evidently had never looked up at the sight of a visitor, but with bent backs pursued their labour. When I went over to see them, they did not prove in the slightest degree communicative. One was an old man who could not be far from the Psalmist's limit of three-score and ten, and the other his grandson. The offer to buy some milk produced the information that they had no women-kind about the place at all, and it was not worth their while to go back to the house for the purpose of selling a pennyworth of milk, though the boy finally consented to do so when the prospect of selling some eggs also was dangled before him. When alone he proved to be more talkative than his grandfather, and from him I learned that the holding was a small one of forty acres, and had belonged to them for two or three generations. The condition of the place was certainly no tribute to the prosperity of that class of person, and, truth to tell, it had little attraction. It served as a striking contrast to the next farm, which I got into by simply crossing a fence.

The latter proved to be a 300-acre farm, rented by a keen and intelligent tenant who looked a little askance when he saw a visitor calmly approaching across a field of young wheat, but who, nevertheless, proved to be perfectly courteous when the situation was explained to him. Here there was no picturesque untidiness. There was scarcely a weed even at the

"ONE WAS AN OLD MAN WHO COULD NOT BE FAR FROM THE PSALMIST'S LIMIT OF THREE-SCORE AND TEN"

hedge roots; the spring crops were put in in the neatest manner imaginable; the farmhouse was, it is true, old but it had been mended and improved till it looked like a villa at Clapham. The farmer appeared to have got through most of his sowing, and as he was going about among his stock himself, he did not at all mind my going with him. His conversation might have

been instructive to anybody who was interested in husbandry, but it was certainly not very poetical. Young lambs gambolling in the meadows led him to no deeper reflection than that "ship," as he called them, were a bad market at the moment, and wool no better. His calves – and prettier creatures no one could wish to see – led to a disquisition on the iniquity of certain middlemen whom he represented as robbing the honest farmer of the profit which should come to him naturally from the sale of milk, and his foals only led to a diatribe against the use of "stinking and dangerous motors." To listen to him one would have thought that bankruptcy or the parish was waiting for him round the corner, and yet I would venture to take a wager that his balance at the bank was not one to be altogether despised.—JOSIAH MARKER

JANUARY 9TH, 1948

PARSONS WHO FARM

SOME TIME AGO I was asked if I knew whether many parsons farm the glebe land that goes with their livings. Today very few parsons are farming their glebe, but one who has done so, the Rev. G. C. N. Webb, Vicar of Southwick cum Boarhunt in Hampshire, gives an interesting account of his experiences. September, 1939, found him in a remote moorland parish where it was not easy to get milk for the children. Neither his wife nor he was accustomed to tending cows, but they were both familiar with the older tradition of the country and judged that it would be possible to slip into the rhythm of the land without too much difficulty.

"MR. WEBB'S FIRST ADVICE IS THAT NO PARSON SHOULD TRY TO FARM HIS GLEBE UNLESS HE IS TOUGH"

Mr. Webb prepared the way by helping neighbouring farmers with their field work and then he asked one of them to teach him to milk. In due course he bought a cow, Primrose, and drove her down to the rectory, housing her in the stables which he had fitted up as a byre. But the doctor brought Mr. Webb's farming activities to a sudden end. He told him bluntly that he could quit his farming or have a coffin. So Mr. Webb's first advice is that no parson should try to farm his glebe unless he is tough.—CINCINNATUS

A TYPICAL JERSEY

*Every now and again, every editor is confronted with something so good
that it's impossible not to put it in gratuitously.*

T HE JERSEY IS unquestionably the most beautiful cow to be seen on
our English pastures. And it is with very great pleasure that we
show today the picture of a very representative specimen. It was
done for quite another purpose by one of our valued contributors, but
the temptation to show it in these pages proved quite irresistible.

DECEMBER 17ᵀᴴ, 1904

A WOLF AMONG THE LAMBS

Within the pages of the magazine are some curious accounts of farming dramas such as this.

As WE WRITE the farmers in Northumberland are having a very exciting time. Not long ago a wolf belonging to a travelling menagerie escaped from its cage, and since then has been having a destructive holiday among the sheep, having killed over a score up to Saturday night. On that day a crowd of 400 people assembled, armed with every kind of firearm, from the ancient flint-gun to the newest choke-bore self-ejector. They located the animal easily enough in a plantation; but it was a more difficult task to deal with it. The beaters went in, and the guns were stationed outside, but after two hours' search they still had sought the wolf in vain. Then came the rumour that it had been viewed crossing the highway not far from Allandale village, and was lurking in the bed of the stream. No sooner did the hunters come up, however, than it broke cover, and sped away with remarkable haste in the direction of the fells. It proved to be much too swift for either horses or dogs. Eventually the scent was lost, and the animal got clear away. It is a matter that causes great anxiety to the flockmasters of the district, as, to say nothing of the actual slaughter, the ewes are getting into that condition in which they cannot be chased and hunted about without grave danger.

> "NOT LONG AGO A WOLF BELONGING TO A TRAVELLING MENAGERIE ESCAPED FROM ITS CAGE"

SEPTEMBER 2ND, 1939

ARP FOR ANIMALS

The war wisdom of Country Life *extended to plugging government literature on animal care. Even London in 1939 supported a vastly greater number of animals than it does today.*

EVERYBODY WHO IS engaged in the care and management of animals should possess a copy of "Air Raid Precautions for Animals," published by the Stationery Office for threepence. In certain areas, such as docks, railway goods depots and some industrial centres, there may be large numbers of transport and other animals, and in cities, of course, there are large numbers of domestic pets. Such areas, it is rightly pointed out, are especially liable to air attack. The booklet shows clearly and concisely what action should be taken and what treatment used in circumstances arising from each and every kind of air attack where animals are concerned. Moreover, it is pointed out that, wherever possible, animals should be evacuated from urban centres as speedily as possible; but in the case of milch cows evacuation is desirable since the difficulties of inward transport of the necessary fodder might be greater than that of the transport of milk from outside areas. Hacks and riding ponies should be moved at once, while dogs and cats and other pets must be considered to be the personal responsibility of their owners.

SEPTEMBER 9ᵀᴴ, 1939

THE PLOUGH IN WAR

Both wars brought about important transformations in farming. Amongst other things, there was an immediate recognition that agricultural production would have to be maximised. Country Life was quick to point out in a leader some of the mistakes that had been made in the First World War as the Second engulfed Britain.

I N ONE WAY war brings a consolation: it involves putting our land to its greatest productive capacity. Under normal conditions in this country the decision whether a farm shall carry its maximum of crops and stock, or mark time with the minimum of outlay, has for twenty years been made, not by the farmer, not even by the Ministry of Agriculture, but by industrial and commercial factors in international exchange. Under war conditions that elaborate system no longer affects Farmer Giles's hundred acres.

The importance of the plough in war-time – as in any productive policy of agriculture – is the greater food-value of its products, not necessarily corn, over that of untreated grassland. The conclusion is that, important as the plough is in the increase of corn supplies, it is of equal, perhaps greater, importance for ensuring meat and the perishable but essential supplies of milk and butter. If the last War had continued a little longer, we should have suffered much more seriously from reduction of milk and meat supplies owing to the lack of shipping tonnage. With the possible restriction of imported feeding-stuffs for cattle, the increase of nutritive pastures of rye grass, clover, sainfoin, lucerne, and kale is vital. The mistake made twenty years ago was not in ploughing-up pastures, but in devoting what had been ploughed-up so exclusively to corn.

THINNING OUT ROOKERIES

EVEN THE STERNEST critic of rooks will admit that in their make-up virtue and vice are pretty evenly balanced. Rooks are industrious and, especially during spring and early summer, capable assistants to the gardener in ridding him of wireworms, leather-jackets, weevils, and the like. On the other hand, they have certain features which the farmer views with a good deal of dismay: witness the bare patches in spring sowings where a colony has got to work, the thatch torn off ricks, and the great gaps in pea and bean fields. The game preserver and the poultry breeder also bear a grudge against rooks as egg thieves of cunning and experience. I have seen rooks combine to drive game off their nests and assemble, carefully gauging the extreme range of a shotgun, and wait until opportunity offered for a raid on the chicks of a pheasant-rearing field. It is true that where their numbers are not excessive such crimes are usually the work of a few individuals of depraved tastes. But in areas where rooks hunt in such vast companies as preclude the possibility of their having sufficient natural food supplies they become a public nuisance. So, quite apart from the vexed question whether rook shooting is entitled to be called a minor sport, it is a necessity in over-populated districts. And it can be effectual, in the sense of thinning rookeries out to reasonable proportions, only if the young rooks are dealt with before they are able to take to wing. For once they can fly they have sense enough to fly at such a height that in all probability they will live out the term of their natural lives without ever giving the most skilful marksman a chance. To describe rook shooting as "massacre of the innocents" is not only sentimentalism carried to excess, but definitely misleading. Properly conducted, it is a more humane way of taking bird life than any other, for a .22 rook rifle has a range greatly in excess of the tallest tree, and if one does not make a clean kill one must of necessity make an equally clean miss. Bullets do not prick or graze like small shot from a shotgun.—J. B. DROUGHT

MAY 9TH, 1931

THE KING'S HERDSMAN

To the Editor of "Country Life."

Sir,—I enclose you a photograph which I took some little time ago, that may interest Country Life readers. It shows Uriah Robbins, the King's herdsman at Sandringham, who on Monday last celebrated his ninetieth birthday and is still hale and hearty. A native of Somerset, he is seen wearing a smock typical of his county. This faithful servant has been on the Sandringham estate over forty years.—G. Parsons

OLD ENGLISH BRANDRETHS

Sometimes Country Life *looked backwards to supply answers to modern problems. Wartime concerns about food consumed or spoilt by rats elicited this suggestion:*

THE GOVERNMENT'S DRIVE against damage by rats should revive the use of these ancient devices. The art of stack thatching has received its due share of attention from writers interested in rural pursuits over many centuries, but the almost equally important stack foundation seems to have been neglected. In the corn-growing districts, permanent structures may often be found in the stack-garths, particularly in the Cotswolds and on the Pennine slopes, where they are known as "brandreys," a term derived from the Anglo-Saxon "brandreth." They vary in form, but the most widespread variety consists of two or three rows of upright supports, about two feet high, bearing flat stone slabs on which the timber foundation rests. These serve the double purpose of keeping the stack dry and preventing the ravages of rats, for, while these versatile little creatures can easily climb the stone pillars, they are unable to walk upside down underneath the stone slabs.

Along the east coast of Scotland and in the north generally a foundation of an entirely different character, known as a bess, truss or stack-centre, is used. This is a pyramidal wooden structure, the purpose of which is to ventilate the stack. As the hot air rises, cool fresh air passes through the base of the stack, a process aided by the stack-centre. When the stack is large, the inroad of fresh air is facilitated by a horizontal structure of a similar nature. Such bosses are constructed of split pine and are usually the work of the village carpenter, although in some districts, where the demand is slight, the farmer will knock his own together.— JAMES WALTON

AUGUST 15ᵀᴴ, 1903

HARVEST AND ITS PROSPECTS

IN YEARS SUCH as this it seems to us that the yellowing of the corn comes as a great surprise. As we grow older the wheel of time, that moved so slowly in the days of youth, begins to whirl round with increasing energy. That is one reason for surprise, but a more commonplace one seems to lie in the nature of recent springs. Winter seems to be ever thrusting itself farther forward into the original domain of its successor, and we have experienced so little fine weather that it appears to be incredible that already more than half the summer is over and gone. Nevertheless our feelings do not alter the facts of Nature, and a long run through the country lanes shows us that, even as we write, and that is some days before printing, the corn is already cut in some places. The oats were taking that beautifully white appearance which is their nearest approach to yellow. The tall wheat was standing as yet in unbroken green, but full eared, and only waiting for a spell of sunshine to begin to change colour. The barley, bearded and

full, was nodding in the wind as if wishing the sun to come out, and the landscape generally had assumed those sober and dark hues that we associate with early autumn.

There is nothing more beautiful in Nature than a field of corn glowing with red poppies, that appear not so much as individuals, but as blending the whole colour of the field into a fine tone of scarlet. Sunshine has more than a golden value. It is necessary to ripen the crops and bring them to perfection. The value of wheat reaped in sunshine, needless to say, is greater than that gathered under any other conditions, and, unlike hay, corn suffers from every shower. A sunny harvest is always not only the most delightful, but the most profitable one.

JULY 11TH, 1903

THE HAYMAKING SEASON

IT IS DOUBTFUL if in any previous years such a number of what appear to be contradictory accounts of the hay harvest have been published. In the South, as far as quantity is concerned, the year must almost prove a record. Reports from Hampshire, Devonshire, Dorsetshire, Berkshire, Worcestershire, Gloucestershire, Herefordshire, Kent, and Essex are all favourable as to the amount of hay grown; but that does not prevent a great deal of it from having been utterly spoiled. Many of the fields were under water for a considerable time in June, and what this means every practical farmer knows. The grass and clover plants become so embedded in clay and earth that self-respecting cattle will not look at them. It is quite impossible that the quality can be up to a high standard, even although the getting in of the hay has been accomplished in beautiful weather.

IN THE VILLAGE

The village, its institutions and its people are endlessly fascinating subjects for the British. In their descriptions, these old articles from Country Life *reflect both the changes and the continuities of village life over the last century or more.*

✦ VIII ✦

THE OFFICES OF "COUNTRY LIFE"   LONDON   THE OFFICES OF "COUNTRY LIFE"

NOVEMBER 26TH, 1932

INN SIGNS

I N RECENT YEARS several movements have been at work to preserve and improve English rural life. Some bodies are trying to protect the face of the countryside from disfigurement, others are reviving and developing traditional crafts, but all must welcome efforts to cherish good old inn signs and to secure good new ones. Anyhow, signs must be well nursed to survive the inevitable exposure to every kind of weather. If discriminating patrons and good craftsmen can more and more be brought together, there will be cause for rejoicing. The issue is not only artistic, for inn signs so often illustrate heraldic features or local traditions which appeal to the antiquarian mind.

TYPICAL ENGLISH VILLAGES

JULY 22ND, 1899   BRAY

THERE ARE A few villages in England that have repute from odd or remarkable happenings in their history. Bray is known all the world over for the nimble shrewdness of its erstwhile vicar, and, wherever Englishmen are, the "Vicar of Bray" is now the very type of ready compliance and apologetic wit. But Bray deserves to be known for much more than the suppleness of the reverend turncoat. Rare picturesqueness and an old-world rusticity, a beautiful church and a quaint hospital, with many charms of our rural England, the orchards gay with blossom in the spring, rich with fruit in the autumn, the broad cornfields, and the cottages wreathed with flowers – all these things has Bray, and the village lies by the bank of ancient Thames. It has been the fortune of Bray to lie upon no highway save the river, and thus much of the old picturesqueness of the village has been preserved.

The church speaks for itself – a typical village church, with a very good tower of flint and chalk, mostly of the Perpendicular period, but illustrating also the Early English and Decorated styles; just one of those churches which have grown with the centuries. The simple stone covering the "vivacious vicar" of Bray may escape a casual survey. This worthy was Simon Alleyn, who died in the memorable year 1588. His vicariate had extended through the reigns of Henry VIII, Edward VI, Mary, and Elizabeth, but whatever change came he stood true. Reproach good Simon Alleyn with being a turncoat or a backslider, and he would reply, "Not so, sir, for I always kept my principle, which is this – to live and die the vicar of Bray!"

179

DECEMBER 6ᵀᴴ, 1946

THE MYSTERY OF THE MUMMERS

IT WAS CERTAINLY in another century and as it seems to me now in another world, that I last witnessed a complete performance of the Mummers' play. The theatre was obviously designed for its purpose and, both inside and outside, the setting was perfect. Outside, the moonlit snow crunched under the foot. Now and again as one of the boys in the choir sidestepped into a drift there would be hoots and shouts of laughter. Old Tom would drop his fiddle. Wet? No, quite dry, but had Mr. Garvice remembered the tuning-fork? Then there was that dratted boy tripping over with the lantern. And then for a few moments there would be something like silence under the stars, except for the soft thuds of snow falling from the trees. Inside the auditorium was being arranged. By the blazing fire on the open hearth stood a long refectory table. Excess of nostalgia forbids me to describe its burden.

A knocking was heard on the door. Nobody seemed to pay attention, but the high treble of a choir boy, ardently pursued by Old Tom's fiddle, piped up a sudden prayer. This was the signal for the irruption, a patter of feet, the door flung wide, and a very boyish voice proclaiming what Sir Edmund Chambers, in a more serious description of the Mummers Play than this, calls the Presentation of the Drama.

Until comparatively recent days it had been a widespread tradition for particular villages to have their bands of mummers who each winter rehearsed a "play" and at Christmas performed it sometimes in the hospitable surroundings of an inn or country house, sometimes, in suitable weather, in the open. The words of the "play" had been handed down, so far as anybody knew, from time immemorial by word of mouth. The players joined the band as youths, played their parts until they left the village, became decrepit or died, and then the part was handed on to a new recruit. Tradition as to the number of characters, their names, their parts and generally in regard to the nature of the "play" itself varied in different parts of the country.—RALPH JEFFERSON

NOVEMBER 22ND, 1902

VILLAGE TYPES

To the Editor of "Country Life."

Sir,—Here is a village type which I venture to think a credit to the land which produced it. It is a very exact portrait of a Sussex labourer, who (although over eighty) has toiled unceasingly from childhood, without once incurring the risks involved in medical attendance. He was employed when a lad as a carrier's assistant, and in that capacity was soaked to the skin with monotonous frequency. On these occasions he had no chance of changing his clothes, but laid down to rest in them in the only available bedroom – the stable for the carrier's horses.

"THERE IS AN INDEFINABLE AIR OF 'YOU BE HANGEDNESS' ABOUT HIM"

Notwithstanding all this, rheumatism and this sturdy old peasant are not even upon bowing terms, while his back remains as flat as the board beside him. He states that he could digest the very substantial boots he exhibits, and is, as a matter of sequence, persistently optimistic. There is, moreover, an indefinable air of "you be hangedness" about him pleasantly suggestive of that county which is supposed to have been the last converted to Christianity.—F.

SEPTEMBER 26TH, 1903

COTTAGE HOMES

TO THE EDITOR OF "COUNTRY LIFE."

SIR,—The accompanying photograph might stand almost as a typical illustration of the proverb among the North Country people, that "every herring hangs by its own head." Typically a Scottish proverb, I think – typical of a county in whose "geological strata," as I read somewhere the other day, "there is no blarney stone" – a people sufficient for themselves, able to take their own responsibilities, to "hang by their own heads." Of course, the obvious comment on this, as one glances at the picture, is that they are not herrings at all that are shown thus capitally dependent – not herrings but haddocks, beautifully redolent and flavoursome of the peat and pine smoke.

All this interior, indeed, we may suppose, with some little confidence, to be fairly flavoursome. There is the cooking pot, and what it may have within who can say? But at least we can say this, that its reek is going up to mingle with a combined scent of drying haddock and of onion, and if this does not seem to be laying good foundations for a nosegay, one is at a loss to know what would. However, the goodman cleaving the wood is for the moment in a state of sublime detachment from all this, neither yielding to its charm, nor finding its strength too overpowering. He is in the self-sufficing mood of concentration on his task that is a sign of the state of one who can "hang by his own head".—H. G.

THE VILLAGE SHOP

WE WERE ONCE called a nation of shopkeepers, and, although there is no reason to think that, at the time when Napoleon or whoever it was made the remark, there were more shops per head of population here than elsewhere, it is still very pleasant to view the quantity of little shops in a picturesque village or market town. They give an air of thriving local life, their proprietors are often valuable citizens, and, in the past, have done much to build up the beauty of our towns and villages and to recruit the strength of the smaller gentry. It is deplorable to see the glaring uniform facia boards of the giant chain stores, against which so many protests have been made in this paper, vulgarising the shopping streets of country towns. But if one overhears the ladies of a household discussing the perennial subject of shopping, sentiment and aesthetics are apt to get a painful shock. These experts do not seem to appreciate the fact that Mr. Chop, the butcher, is the sixth of his family to do business from that fine old Georgian house; that Honey, grocer and sundriesman, is a churchwarden and a delight to chat with across the counter; or even that Sarsnet and Save, that excellent drapery and general business, is one of the largest ratepayers in the town. They are preoccupied with sordid questions of price, quality, and variety of choice, and only too often seem to prefer, on those grounds, the big business interlopers or, even worse, to have things delivered by van from London. The moral is that individual traders, if they are to preserve their individuality and their trade, must themselves get together for co-operative buying, specialisation, and the weeding out of redundancy, as producers are doing both in industry and agriculture. It is not only in the world of art that machinery has killed the individual craftsman. Long may the village shop survive; but to do so it must move with the times.

A BERKSHIRE SHEEP FAIR

O N LEAVING THE station the road winds sharp up a steep hill. The sloping meadows with high hedges and tall, shaggy elms are soon left behind, and the summit of the hill reveals one of those characteristic hedgeless Berkshire landscapes. You drive through ripening cornfields which run to the foot of the downs. These fill the horizon from left to right, "like a greyhound in full career," as Mr. Meredith has somewhere expressed it.

It is a beautiful open country, but silent, lonely, and deserted. For miles there is not a village in sight; not a vehicle of any description, not even a dusty cyclist to break the monotony of the long white road, which seems to lead nowhere. Occasionally there is a wayside inn by a cross-road or a half dry dew-pond, which serves to water the flocks that pasture on the hills. On and on it goes, now dipping into a hollow, now rising on to a ridge, till at last, after many milestones have been passed, a village, snug in the hollow of the downs and half hidden in an isolated and unexpected island of green, comes into sight. Looking down from the top of the hill everything looks motionless and quiet. It is not until the

first few cottages are passed and the central street is reached that the surge and noise break suddenly upon you. It is like a living sea of life, a waveless yellow sea all spotted with black heads, and the ceaseless moan of that sea is the ceaseless bleating of sheep, and the shrill sharp barking of dogs, and the continued shouting of shepherds. Right to the top of the hill, on either side of the road, against the walls of the cottages, up the side streets, into the adjoining meadows, the sheep are crowded and penned. By ten in the morning the village is a seething, living mass. By three there is neither man nor beast to be seen; the village street is deserted, only the empty pens remaining to show what thousands of living creatures have passed that way

> "IT IS LIKE A LIVING SEA OF LIFE, A WAVELESS YELLOW SEA ALL SPOTTED WITH BLACK HEADS, AND THE CEASELESS MOAN OF THAT SEA IS THE CEASELESS BLEATING OF SHEEP"

for a few short hours. Many miles of dusty road these flocks must travel, for they come from all the villages, farms, and towns around, to this lonely village in the hollow of the downs. Then there are the auctioneers and dealers "from Lunnun," and farmers of every size, shape, and description: the benevolent old-fashioned type with side whiskers and wide-awake hat; the smart young yeoman in his towny jacket suit; the alert, shrewd, and rather "horsey" sheep-dealer, who puts up at the best inn and drinks champagne for lunch. There are shepherds old and young, some still surprisingly picturesque in this twentieth century of ours, with sun-faded clothes and tanned, weatherbeaten faces, suggestive of the long hours passed on lonely hills in all seasons and in all weathers.

SEPTEMBER 10TH, 1959

A POLEMIC AGAINST HEDGES

BY GEOFFREY GRIGSON

A NEIGHBOUR OF mine in Wiltshire has lately added a piece of meadow to his garden – a sensible neighbour, if he will allow me to say so, except at times.

He showed me the addition. I admired the new distance, the wych elm over the long, flat field, the new sense of freedom, in a garden which now seemed part of the wider landscape; and was feeling how excellent it would be to sit here and drink in the evenings, my neighbour now extending himself (and myself with him, I hoped, since his company and his liquor are good) for miles beyond a mere boundary into a green distance.

"A tall hedge . . ."

I didn't quite hear at first.

"A tall hedge," remarked my neighbour a second time. He was going to plant, across the view, this autumn, *a tall hedge*.

I said he wasn't. He said he was. Six feet high. He was going, I said, to shut distance out, himself in; the wych elm out, his family in; freedom out, servitude in, with the aid of a tall green hedge, 6 ft. high. I argued. And there the matter stood – or stands – for a while. But this neighbour of mine reads COUNTRY LIFE, and if this number isn't smuggled away from him, distance, and wych elm, and freedom in his new garden may have had their last chance. Why – this had brought my kettle at last to the boil – are we so dotty on hedges? On walls? I admit a hedge or a wall in a garden, in the right place, around the house, may do visual wonders; but not all around. Why must we have brick and concrete block, and privet and box and thorn and yew and beech and *Lonicera nitida*, and other opacities, so close about us, everywhere?

Why is England shut away, so much of it, behind ridiculous road hedging? Who started it? And again why?

The answer, I suppose, could be historical, or it could be psycho-analytical, or both. Historians show villages without hedges, mediaeval ones, I mean. They show cottages which stand about in a hedgeless, sociable nakedness. So house-hedges, close garden hedges, are modern?

And very slowly, it seems to me, very slowly, but certainly, through the centuries, these walls, these hedges, these restrictions and these strangulators of vision, these hands around the spiritual throat, these claustro-horrors, have been closing in, till earth or stone turns to privet and iron railings intermingled.

To the Editor of "Country Life."

Sir,—Surely we shall not all agree with Geoffrey Grigson's article. One can sympathise wholeheartedly with his annoyance at the six-foot-high hedge to block an apparently open vista, but unfortunately houses commanding such views are nowadays comparatively few. More frequently one's windows overlook a housing estate, a road or a neighbour's garden, and consequently hedges predominate in these circumstances because they act as wind barriers, tend to reduce noise of traffic, shut out the eyesores and form a background to the garden (who likes to see a herbaceous border against a distant line of washing or television aerials?), give one the enjoyment of privacy, keep in livestock and keep out trespassers. Pull down ill-kept field hedges by main roads, yes; but what about country lanes? Would such a lane in, say, early summer, with the hawthorn in blossom, have an appeal of equal aesthetic value to a strip of tarmac bordered by the inevitable barbed-wire fence? I think not.—T. Martin Trowell

JUNE 22ND, 1910

ROUND THE VILLAGE PUMP

The magazine is almost never overtly political and elections, therefore, rarely feature in its pages. Here is an exception, a commentary voiced in so patrician a tone as to be almost unthinkable today.

IT HAS BEEN highly amusing in the strictly rural and agricultural parishes to study the effect of the General Election on the minds of the labourers and their wives and children. Perhaps the particular village is exceptionally ignorant, and politics as politics never seem to be argued about by the people themselves. Like the little girl in *Punch*, they regard the coming of a General Election much as they might have done the arrival of a circus. Rich people and those in trade may regret the check to activity incidental to it; thinkers may have grave doubts and anxieties as to the derision the country may arrive at; but these and other perplexities of the well-to-do and the intelligent do not even pass like shadows over the minds of our rustics. Their work goes on exactly the same during a political contest as at any other time, and having little to lose either way, they are not burdened with anxiety as to the issue. In the political club one hears the philosopher from his armchair expounding the manner in which the rural population look at the question,

generally assuming that the labourer is considering what will give him work or what will give him wages, or conduce to his comfort and so forth.

"IT IS A PLEASURE TO SPEAK TO THEM, BECAUSE THEY ARE UNCONTAMINATED BY NEWSPAPER READING"

This argues a forethought of which little trace can be found in the cottages.

Of course, it is possible and even probable that all the cottagers are not as simple as they look, and that they hold opinions without caring to make the fact public. This sort of reticence seems to be a natural part of the rural character.

Some day it will be worthwhile to make an enquiry into this typical village in order to find out what proportion of the men are unable to read and write and have still to make their signature by mark. That there are a considerable number in this position is well known to the writer, and it has to be said, too, that the illiterate are in their own way the most intelligent. One, a shepherd, cannot repeat the letters of the Alphabet, yet he understands sheep and dogs as very few understand them. By a coincidence the man who inhabits the cottage next to him is a stock keeper, whose education has been similarly neglected. He cannot read or write either, and yet during the thirty-five years he has taken care of his employer's horses he has never made a mistake with them. On politics the minds of both are a complete blank. It is a pleasure to speak to them, because they are uncontaminated by newspaper reading, and as far as I know they never have any desire to hear the newspaper read.—O.

MAY 21ST, 1910

OLD PUBLIC HOUSE GAMES

O F LATE YEARS the tendency of the local authorities has been to suppress these altogether, under the idea that they form additional attractions to the public house. This may be so in town, where the working man who has money to spend congregates, but in the country places, where the labourer cannot afford to spend more than a few pence daily out of his income of fifteen shillings a week, the rule operates harshly, and removes some of the very little interest from the dull bucolic life.

Nine-men's morris was more often played by shepherds and others on the turf – Shakespeare talks of the "nine men's morris is filled up with mud" – but sometimes indoors on a board. Other games were akin to the Toad in the Hole, in which a large image of a toad with wide-open mouth was screwed to a table, and the player threw discs of copper into the mouth. Ninepins, later on called skittles, (which is a corruption of kettle or kittle-pins), no doubt originated from the old game of cayles, in which the objects aimed at were like small sugarloaves arranged in a long row broadside on to the player, who threw at them with a stick.

THE ANNALS OF THE PARISH

IN THE MORNING paper there is no column more diligently studied than that devoted to births, marriages, and deaths, and perhaps it is an interest akin to this that makes us linger over the pages of old parish registers. The clerks in holy orders, who used to keep them in days gone by, were not so much afflicted by the spirit of formalism as are those of our day. The registrar of the modern parish is an official whose record must be entered under

> "THE SPIRIT OF SCEPTICISM WAS KILLING THE ANCIENT BELIEF IN SORCERY"

certain headed columns which give him no opportunity of airing his own individuality or of telling us anything particular about the persons whose names are set down. This was not always the case.

At a time when astrology was absolutely believed in, the parson evidently recorded the baptism with a view to the horoscope of the child being subsequently cast. From Brandish in Suffolk, in the year 1600, we get the following example of this type of entry :

"THE XXVJTH DAIE OF OCTOBER WAS BAPTISID THOMAS COLBYE THE SONNE OF THOMAS COLBYEGENT AND ANNYE UX BEEINGE BORNE THE XIIJ DAIE OF OCTOBER THE SIGNE BEEINGE IN TAURUS AT THE HOWER OF VIJ OF THE CLOCKE IN THE EVENINGE."

This belief of course persisted down to very recent years. It will be remembered that Sir Walter Scott makes use of it as an everyday incident when Colonel Mannering, who had dabbled in the mystic science, cast the horoscope of young Ellen Gower; but that was towards the end of the eighteenth century, and already the Spirit of scepticism was killing the ancient belief in sorcery.

3

JUNE 6ᵀᴴ, 1931

VILLAGE CROSSES

To the Editor of "Country Life."

Sir,—Village crosses, market crosses and churchyard crosses are scattered widely all over the land, but this one at St. James Deeping is notable in that it fulfils three functions. One is that it is all that is left of a superb Perpendicular cross. The style places it in the reign of either Henry V or Henry VI. Is it a question for antiquarians to decide whether the Abbey of Crowland erected it or the Abbey of Peterborough. There seems just a possibility that the former abbey erected it as marking the abbey bounds. The Crowland monks were partial to large buildings, as witness the triangular bridge which is said, on good authority, to be the giant base of a cross. Whether it was the Puritans who destroyed the main part, or if it was due to the malignancy of the Reformation, is not on record. The fact that the base was made into the town gaol rather points to Puritan hands. Taken all round, the base is certainly unique. It is open to question if in all England there is another like it. It is to be hoped that it will be registered as a historical monument, otherwise there is always the danger that it will be removed to make room for some modern atrocity. The lamp is, of course, a deplorable feature.—F. J. E.

TO PREVENT BODY-SNATCHING

The country churchyard enjoys a very special place in British sensibilities.
Here the living can wander in pleasant contemplation of the past, its people
and some of its more curious practices.

To the Editor of "Country Life."

Sir,—In the churchyard of the charming old Saxon church of Warblington, Hampshire, there are two watchers' huts, the purpose of which was the prevention of body-snatching from the graves. These are in the north-west and south-east corners of the churchyard thus commanding a view of the whole place. Each is about 7 ft. square, and has a fireplace. The church is in an isolated position, and quite near the harbour coast. A relative of the former rector has a relic in the form of a badge (of which I enclose a sketch) worn by the watchers. This is a silver disc about 2 ½ ins. in diameter, heavily embossed with oak leaves. I understand that it was worn on the arm with a leather band, in the same manner as that of a special constable.—M. Stafford Cooke (mrs.)

SILVER BADGE WORN BY THE
GRAVE-WATCHERS AT WARBLINGTON,
HAMPSHIRE

COUNTRY CHURCHYARD

THE SNOW HAD ceased to fall. A few last flakes yet floated in the pale light of the winter sun. The narrow country road winding on before me at last lifted and passed over the crest of the hill. And here, solitary, overlooking the valley, stood the dark, snowy tower of a country churchyard. A robin began to sing as I turned aside and entered the lich-gate. Not a sound broke the beautiful stillness; not a figure, man nor beast, moved across these reaches of new-fallen snow. Pale light and coloured shadow played in hollow and ripple. Melancholy and foreboding were rare in these old legends. It is not the being dead that matters, but the having lived. It was bitterly cold in spite of the quiet air. Yet who could forbear brushing the bright snow away to read, bejewelled with rime, poor Tom Logge's candid summing-up?

HERE LIES THOMAS LOGGE • A RASCALLY DOGGE
A POOR USELESS CREATURE • BY CHOICE AS BY NATURE
WHO NEVER SERVED • GOD FOR KINDNESS NOR ROD
WHO NEVER DID ANY • FOR PLEASURE NOR PENNY
WORK IN HIS LIFE • BUT TO MARRY A WIFE
AND LIVE AYE IN STRIFE :
AND ALL THIS HE SAYS • AT THE END OF HIS DAYS
LEST SOME FINE CANTING PEN • SHOULD BE AT HIM AGAIN.

That "pen," I am afraid, is still extant, a plume of the Phoenix, though this "rascally dogge" seems to have been in no great danger from it here.

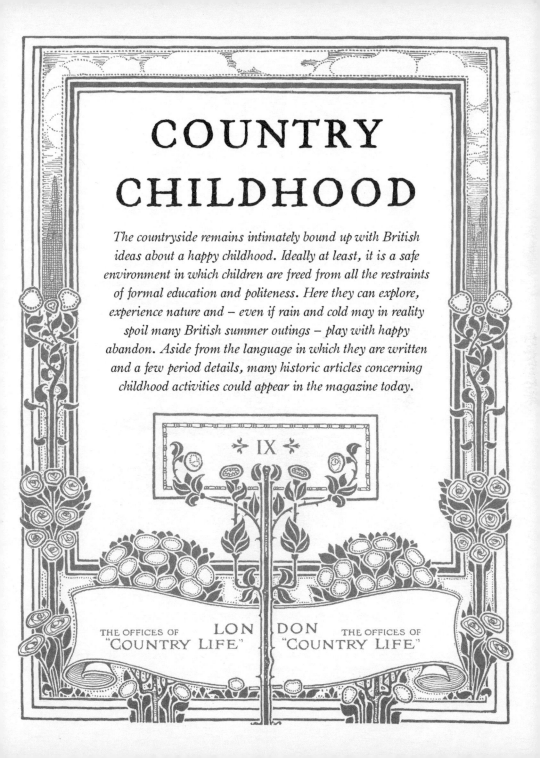

COUNTRY
CHILDHOOD

The countryside remains intimately bound up with British ideas about a happy childhood. Ideally at least, it is a safe environment in which children are freed from all the restraints of formal education and politeness. Here they can explore, experience nature and – even if rain and cold may in reality spoil many British summer outings – play with happy abandon. Aside from the language in which they are written and a few period details, many historic articles concerning childhood activities could appear in the magazine today.

✣ IX ✣

THE OFFICES OF   LONDON   THE OFFICES OF
"COUNTRY LIFE"   "COUNTRY LIFE"

AUGUST 2ND, 1902

SEASIDE JOYS

ISTANT WHITE CLIFFS and green downs running inland from their crest as far as eye can reach; the yellow riband of sand, barred at intervals with green-black groynes, rough with mussels and fringed with green laver and black bladder wrack; blue-grey sea, flecked with breakers, meeting the yellow sand-riband on one horizon and the blue sky on another; the faint blur of distant smoke from ocean-going steamers; the shimmering July sun, and seven laughing youngsters – what more can you want to complete a picture of perfect happiness? Bare-legged, half-clad, hand in hand, they stream across the level stretch of sand towards the groyne. Perhaps if grown-ups elected to sit – as, you may be sure, they never would – upon anything so clammy, and at the same time so prickly, as a barnacled groyne, they would choose its landward end, where at least they could plant their feet upon the shingle. But childhood has other notions, and to dangle bare legs over rippling water

"WHAT MORE CAN YOU WANT TO COMPLETE A PICTURE OF PERFECT HAPPINESS?"

has an added charm when balancing feats are needed to reach the slippery perch. It is not rudeness which makes most of them roar with laughter because an elder sister has screamed and tip-toed, with gathered skirts, up the beach to escape three inches of water. It is the conscious superiority of youth, which would as soon as not stand upon its head in a rock-pool full of crabs. We have all been young; but, alas!

"WE HAVE ALL BEEN YOUNG; BUT, ALAS! WE CAN ONLY BE YOUNG ONCE"

we can only be young once. The sea has, however, one advantage. It levels all paltry distinctions between bathing drawers. After one dip, even the home-made garment, which was so long in the waist and so slack in the steerage, assumes the proper degrees of clinging tightness; and, even were it otherwise, the captured sea creatures which you hand to your friend will tickle his palm just as nicely whether his bathing drawers sag or no. At the ages of eight and ten you can afford to let your elder sister have a monopoly of thinking whether her bathing costume fits. You bathe: she dresses the part.

COTTAGE CHILDREN'S PASTIMES

IN CERTAIN MOODS one is inclined to think that no money is squandered to less purpose than that which is devoted to the purchase of expensive toys for children, especially very young children. To his young eyes the difference between, say, tin and gold is merely one of colour, therefore expensiveness of material does not concern him in the slightest, and the amusement he derives from a toy is quite independent of the cost. A thing picked up by the roadside may be worth more in his eyes than the most beautiful device that can be purchased from a shop. But the very poor child is thrown entirely on its own resources, and from that very fact obtains more amusement than the rich. Take the example of a sailing-boat. The cottage boy's navigation is rendered much more interesting by the mere circumstance of his being penniless. For one thing, it places him under the necessity of constructing his own navy. There is not much building about it at first. He finds a sea in the nearest brook, and a morsel of bark with a feather for sail will give him amusement enough at a certain stage. It is a singular fact that a lad coming from the country to the town can, in a very short time, pick up all that town has to teach him, but unless the lore of the country be gathered in youth it must remain forever an undiscovered land.

OCTOBER 1ˢᵀ, 1921

OUT ALL NIGHT

A S SCHOOL CLOSED one Friday afternoon I asked the boys: "Who would like to stay out all night with me tomorrow and go home to breakfast on Sunday morning?" Every hand felt for the ceiling. "Very well; meet me at the fountain under Orrest Head at 8.45 p.m., each boy having his parents' permission in the form of a note, at least six large sandwiches, and a cup." At 8.45 the following evening I turned up at the fountain in my very worst clothes and examined the grub and the notes of the thirty boys present. All the notes seemed genuine, so we cast restraint aside and rattled up the Elleray Woods, passed the Professor's cottage, and cast anchor in a beautiful spot under four huge oaks. "Let each boy put his coat and bag on the ground here, and make a big ring with the fire in the centre. Four large stones for the fireplace, so! The small boys please collect wood and twigs, and the older boys come with me and help me 'treacle' the trees." I carried the treacle-pot and brush, and the lads lit the lanterns to help matters. Alongside a path for about half a mile each oak and ash was striped with a mixture of treacle and pear essence. (Rum is better, but it is frightfully wicked to use rum or even to mention it before small boys, especially on a dark night.) Forty trees were branded as a bait for the moths, and as we walked back to the camp fire for supper the lamplight made beautiful play over the glistening blobs of treacle on my very worst clothes.

"Stop! Stop! the dawn! Collect everything, put on coats, stamp the fire flat, and be ready to trek. Line up to be counted. One short? Good gracious! Jimmy Thompson lying fast asleep under the wall in all this noise. Come on, James, far, far away. Silence now!" The light rapidly increased and we soon reached the great swamp among the birches.

Thrushes rubbed their eyes and blinked at us in astonishment, as did the pheasants sitting on the old fence. Rabbits forgot to run in their surprise at seeing such a silent procession of ghosts invading their territory so early in the morning. At last the summit was reached, and we watched the sun rise out of the north-east in a very ordinary fashion. No golden beams, but a plain white rise, with the red ball only partly visible between the horizontal clouds. "But it's Sunday morning, and we'd better be off to breakfast"; so having counted the other lively lads six times and got a different answer each time, I bade them all "Good-morning" and rushed home through the woods lest anyone should see me in my very worst clothes.—Rufus H. Mallinson

SEPTEMBER 14TH, 1912

A FARM FOR BOY SCOUTS

A NOVEL SCHEME AND HOW IT IS WORKED

In the early twentieth century, the countryside was viewed by some as much more than a place of delight; experience of it could also serve the great imperial endeavour.

A NEW "BACK to the land" scheme for Boy Scouts has recently been initiated at Wadhurst, a somewhat obscure village in the East Sussex uplands. It is a farm colony conceived on republican lines for Boy Scouts. They hold the view that when a boy becomes a Scout, the work of scoutcraft should not only be an occupation for his spare time, but should be his only work. And often they have thought what they might make of their boys if they could have them wholly to themselves for, say, the two crucial years from fifteen to seventeen. In that time they could teach them at least one trade thoroughly and something of half-a-dozen other trades, besides giving that magnificent training in character, self-reliance and good citizenship which is the raison d'etre of the Scout Movement. Sir Robert Baden-Powell, the Chief Scout, has been emphasising the growing scarcity of British farm-hands and the difficulties of food production at home; he is anxious to foster in the rising generation a love for the land, and to train the lads to become expert agriculturists at home and in the Colonies. It is intended that the Boy Scouts, while being taught the duties of citizenship on the Baden-Powell principles and receiving the benefits of a modern curriculum, shall be trained in a variety of agricultural pursuits. Thus they are taught how to milk a cow, shoe and ride a horse, bake bread, grow fruit, keep bees, and such handicrafts as carpentry, building, leatherwork and the rudiments of engineering. For proficiency in all of these subjects the usual Scout proficiency badges are awarded after the passing of certain rather severe tests. Had these Boy Scouts never been brought under the influence of Sir Robert Baden-Powell's wonderful scheme, they would have drifted into "blind-alley" occupations, van and messenger boys, and never have lifted up their eyes to the far horizons of lands, more youthful and more hopeful than poor old England.

MARCH 31ST, 1934

PONIES FOR CHILDREN

Though the countryside might offer sober experience for the future builders of empire, the magazine generally gave more emphasis to more engaging children's activities. The pleasures of riding and the chase, for example, were one obvious focus of interest.

FAR AND AWAY the most important point in selecting our pony is to find one of the right temperament. Make and shape are as nothing compared with this. We must find a pony who is perfectly quiet, and yet is not a slug. Sluggish ponies are no good. The child cannot get them along, and therefore he gets bored. Keen ponies are far more often to be met with; they are frequently to be found both among the thoroughbred and the moorland types; and the over-keen pony must be carefully guarded against, for it is this sort of pony which makes a child nervous.

A good many people seem curiously indifferent to the danger of falls. But good teachers are of a different opinion; they believe that if the pony is right and the teacher knows his business, accidents can be almost entirely avoided. The danger of accidents lies not so much in physical damage as in damage to nerve which may be irreparable. In the show-ring accidents are far too frequent; children are too often sent into the ring on ponies which are quite unsuited to them. I have seen a child run away with, another bucked off, another kicked by her own pony, another with a pony who reared, and so on. If a little girl bucked off before hundreds of spectators consequently takes a dislike to riding, can we wonder at it? In seeking to steer clear of any risk of nervousness, we cannot pay too careful attention to the choice of a pony with the right temperament, and, having found him, we must see to it that he never gets too fresh.

OCTOBER 19TH, 1912

BOYS' AND GIRLS' HUNTERS

As I LOOKED over pictures of children's hunters, I could not help thinking that the young people of the present day are more fortunate than their elders were, for these ponies are indeed miniature hunters, as good in their way as the big show hunters which we see in the ring. In past days boys and girls were often sent out on rough ponies for a few weeks under the tuition of the coachman, and then left to shift for themselves. The ponies generally knew more than their riders, and often took their own way without much regard to the bridle. They taught us to ride, they taught us to fall, and we learned to stick on and enjoyed ourselves immensely; but we did not become horsemen and horsewomen in the same sense as many of the boys and girls I see in the hunting-field nowadays. We picked up some bad habits. For example, the hard-mouthed ponies taught us, or encouraged us, to hold on by the bridle. The way we were taught to ride accounts for the bad hands many men and women of the older generation certainly have. Some people will not allow children to go out hunting until their education in the saddle is complete. On the contrary, the sooner a boy or girl can go out with the hounds the better. The excitement and interest of the hunting-field give the young folk confidence, self-reliance and resource, such as they can never attain on the road. Let children begin early, for the habit of horsemanship is a valuable acquisition.—T. F. DALE

"THEY TAUGHT US TO RIDE, THEY TAUGHT US TO FALL"

OCTOBER 11TH, 1902

SPORTS OF CHILDHOOD

LITTLE FRANK LIVES with his father and mother in a secluded farmhouse. It is no wonder that the boy took early to sport, it was his father's hobby, and the farm has every facility for it. A delightful brook, with flowery weed-grown banks, runs unsteadily between meadows of grass to a deep river. Here and there it is crossed by plank bridges, not so big but that Frank could sit stride-legs and watch the speckled trout below him. The boy longed to catch them. What stirred him the more was that at the farm there was a boy called Danny who knew how to do it. Now all the fathers and mothers pointed a finger of warning at Danny. They said he was never out of mischief, and would do no good, but for catching and killing things there was not his equal. Even staid men could not help admiring him, especially those who came from the town to fish.

Frank, bending eagerly over the plank, looked out for the biggest trout, and gently brought the worm close to its mouth. He noticed that some of the others whisked about as if they were in terror, but the large one remained perfectly still except for fanning the water gently with its fins. Frank twitched and guided the line till it was almost in its mouth. The trout turned quickly on its tail and darted away down stream like some dark flying bird. However, he tried again from the reedy bank, he pulled up his line quick, and great was his delight to find he had hooked his first fish, a beautiful red-finned perch. Even Danny condescended to praise him, then he laughed at Frank for trying to catch them with a big lob-worm, which was fit only for the coarse palate of an eel or a perch. Danny set forth his boyish lore till they came to a place where the brook widened over a stony channel with here and there a deeper hole. Danny began "guddling," that is, feeling under the stones and catching them with his hand. No sooner did Frank see him actually catch one or two than he followed his example, and the boys forgot all about time and how the sunny hours were flying, so deeply immersed were they in this pastime.

SEPTEMBER 3RD, 1910

BY KINDNESS

The delight that children find in animals could as easily be diverted
towards managing livestock as hunting it.

To the Editor of "Country Life."

Sir,—In order that you may see what can be done with animals by kindness I enclose two photographs which speak for themselves. My children are eleven years and ten years old respectively, and the sheep are not quite eighteen months old. The sheep have been broken to harness by the children only. They will trot and gallop in the road or in the garden, are quiet to all road nuisances and all are perfectly happy together.—
William H. Back

AUGUST 14TH, 1937

THE BRANCH LINE

EFORE I WAS twelve I had gone far enough along the envied path of becoming an engine driver to be satisfied that I had reached the end of it. About half a mile from home was a station on the double track line that ran through our part of the country, and from it ran a single track branch line to a small town eight miles away. The whole line had a domestic sort of air, as though the driver and guard, and the signalmen-stationmasters, ran it for a hobby. The engine was a stocky little tank engine, I knew every inch of it, every scratch on the paint, the idiosyncrasy of every lever, I worshipped it in my dreams, and longed above all things to possess it. The driver's name was Chris, the fireman's Tom. I developed a routine that I kept to as if it had been an important ritual. I used to go down to the station to meet the little train as it came in, climb up on the footplate, though never without being asked. Climbing up there was a wonderful excitement, and I can believe that no lover of incense has ever found the mystery and satisfaction in its perfume that I found in the mingled smell of oil and steam that filled the whole cabin. Chris would sometimes say "Now you can start her if you like." Then I took the great lever at the side, polished and worn by hard hands, and with his help, let it over; and with my hands on the hot, smooth regulator I would push it across, going faster and faster. So we came to the signal box, where I would pull the little handle of the whistle, and make a loud shriek as we passed, and wave. Then, as Tom and Chris drank their cold tea they used to give me one of their cans to drink from, and a hunk of their bread and cheese, cut with a great clasp knife. That shared meal had sacramental quality for me; and no drink I have ever tasted since has been so good as that cold tea, no food as perfect as that bread and yellow cheese.—CHRISTOPHER WHITFIELD

APRIL 22ND, 1903

POULTRY-KEEPING FOR GIRLS

THERE IS NO more delightful amusement for girls living in the country than the keeping of poultry. The management and rearing of chickens and ducks provide a continual source of interest, as the business must be thoroughly gone into if success is to be attained. The work never grows monotonous, as there are always new birds growing up, and it is a great source of pleasure to watch the little birds changing from soft balls of fluff into fine sturdy chickens. Poultry-work is not work that can be taken up enthusiastically for a few weeks and then forgotten, all through the year the birds require care and attention. The whole business, however, can quite well be taken in hand by girls, the only help that they will probably want being from the yard-man in the thorough cleaning out of the houses. It is far more satisfactory for girls who intend going in for poultry-work to keep their fowls absolutely separate from those of the ordinary household, as otherwise confusion is inevitable; the hens and chickens get mixed up, and no-one can tell positively whose are the eggs, or which hens are laying regularly. As a beginning, Plymouth Rocks, Minorcas, Brahmas, and Dorkings will be found good all-round fowls, and afterwards any special breed can be selected at pleasure. Minorcas and Dorkings are excellent laying hens, and if properly fed and cared for will lay practically all the year round. The great secret in making hens lay all the year round is to feed them properly. They do not want a quantity of food at a time, but a fair amount at regular intervals, and that food carefully prepared. Scraps from the house, potatoes, bread, and meal can be mixed up together, but in the winter months the food should be given hot, and in wet weather a little hemp seed occasionally is an excellent thing.—MARV E. HEZLET

FEBRUARY IST, 1902

WINCHESTER COLLEGE IN 1902

BY AN OLD WYKEHAMIST

The activities of all England's great public schools have been covered in the magazine. Accounts of these institutions, however, are generally supplied from the perspective of the school hierarchy. Here is an old-boy account.

TO AN OLD Wykehamist, it is a matter for pride and pleasure alike that the Editor of COUNTRY LIFE should ask for an article about the place which was the making of him for good or for evil, sauntering through college and gossiping by the way. Through Outer Gate we pause to enter Porter's Lodge – it was the custom to name the successive occupants of the post after the minor prophets – but it is on passing into Chamber Court that we are in the heart of Wykehamical life. Here every stone is full of memories. Chamber Court, entered by way of Middle Gate, is bounded on three sides by buildings of rough flint with stone mullions, and on the fourth by the noblest chapel that it ever entered into the mind of collegiate architect to conceive. Round the four sides and across the middle runs a broad pavement of flagstones, called "Sands," much used for pacing to and fro on summer evenings. The intervening space is paved with a mixture of flints and cobbles. Tradition has it that during the Great Rebellion the original flints were extracted for use as missiles. The reference here is not to the trifling differences between Charles I and Cromwell, but to the far more important affair of 1793, an outbreak in college which cost Dr. Warion his office and thirty-five scholars their places. Next comes the kitchen, where in the entrance stands the famous Trusty Servant. His origin is lost in antiquity, but he was there in the sixteenth century. His present livery was painted on to him in 1798, when George III visited college. The pig's snout indicates freedom from daintiness, the donkey's ears patience and endurance, the padlock reticence, the stag's feet swiftness of foot – on the whole, a perfect treasure of a servant. The flight of steps beyond the kitchen takes us up to hall, which, if somewhat bare and cheerless, is of fine proportions. In it are spread the plain but sufficient meals of seventy boys every day. Immediately below hall is seventh chamber, covered with "marbles" – small tablets bearing the names and dates of entry and departure of bygone scholars of Winchester for hundreds of years past. On one of these is a red mark called Bloody Hand, held by legend to commemorate a murder. And here, having taken the reader quite far enough, I will try to forget that in the seventies we sometimes thought the wandering old Wykehamist tiresome, unless he had taken steps to propitiate us with offerings of cake and ices.

TRENCH DIGGING BY CADETS

*There is particular poignancy in reading articles about generations of
children whose lives were later to be overwhelmed by war. Here public
schoolboys practise for a type of warfare that would probably claim most
of their lives.*

IT IS A great mistake to suppose that the question of entrenchments
is one that concerns only engineers and line battalions; and in giving
a short account of the trenches dug during the last summer term by
the Monkton Combe School Cadet Corps I should like to lay emphasis,
not only on the importance of earthworks, which every military critic
will acknowledge, but also on the interest attaching to this branch of
military science.

I should say, first of all, that the corps is an infantry and not an
engineering company, and from beginning to end the work was entirely
voluntary. There was no organised system of reliefs as laid down in the
military engineering manuals, since the cadets would turn to the work at
odd times with pick and shovel when cricket was over. The digging was
not done in uniform, but in the plainest of plain clothes; in fact, football
shorts and old flannels were generally found to be most suitable. The
site was selected, not from a strategic point of view, but because it was
the only piece of land available for the purpose, and consisted of some
rough ground lying between the cricket-field and the Midford Brook.
The photograph gives a general view of the tire-trench from the rear. It is
divided into sections by traverses to protect the defenders from enfilade
fire, and to localise the effect of bursting shells. All the loopholes were
screened by pieces of canvas sewn on to the sandbags in order to prevent
the light from shining through the loopholes and thus giving away the
position of the trenches. Further to the left was a protected look-out
for the commanding officer, giving a good view of the field of fire in all
directions.—E. G. H.

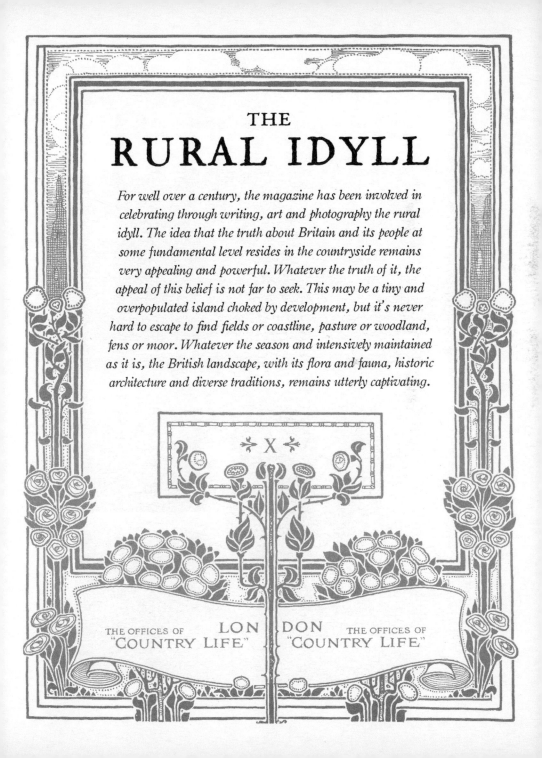

THE
RURAL IDYLL

For well over a century, the magazine has been involved in celebrating through writing, art and photography the rural idyll. The idea that the truth about Britain and its people at some fundamental level resides in the countryside remains very appealing and powerful. Whatever the truth of it, the appeal of this belief is not far to seek. This may be a tiny and overpopulated island choked by development, but it's never hard to escape to find fields or coastline, pasture or woodland, fens or moor. Whatever the season and intensively maintained as it is, the British landscape, with its flora and fauna, historic architecture and diverse traditions, remains utterly captivating.

X

THE OFFICES OF   LONDON   THE OFFICES OF
"COUNTRY LIFE"   "COUNTRY LIFE"

AN INVITATION

Country-Life, clear skies, debonair surroundings,
Poetic silence, solitude reposeful
In common Nature's venerated aspect;
                         And budding indoors

My neglected garden of all the Muses :
Tell me what London giveth or receiveth;
If pleasure hold you, or a duty brighten
                         her sooty mansions.

Few the years now ere the machine betray us
In the long tumult, whether it be heart-stroke
Or flagging brain that deliver the word of
                         weary surrender.

So come, ere fragrant summer undelaying
From river-side and woody glen departeth,
And the shorten'd days hurry on the misty
                         mantle of autumn:

While yet at random to recline agree-eth
On shadow'd bank or sunny lawn, revolving
All the afternoon any joy that art or
                         wisdom accordeth:

Now a-down Thames freighting a skiff to wander
By lock and weir and rushy islet, oaring
His willow-border'd, lily-paven and white-
                         flowery waters.

ROBERT BRIDGES, 1904

JUNE 17TH, 1911

BY LEAFY WAYS

WHILE IT IS extremely pleasant to amble along on the back of a nag, it is also delightful to be whizzed along a country road at the rate of an *express* train. Tenderness for his steed does not need to trouble the man who travels by motor. When he comes to an inn he need not feel the anxieties which continually worry the traveller who answers to the ancient adage that a merciful man is merciful to his steed, and who must see that his horses are properly put up and fed. However, the owner of a motor cannot altogether dispense with an oversight of his carriage. It may not suffer pain, but, nevertheless, it is subject to as many ailments as any quadruped. If it is not fed with oats, it has to be fed with petrol. Where the horseman has the advantage over the motorist is in the character of the country he can traverse. We have been turning over in our mind what districts would be best for our equestrian tourist. There are many districts in Great Britain where the tourist on horseback might enjoy solitude and beautiful scenery. These are, broadly speaking, the mountain districts, where the heathery moor stretches wide on either side and there is no noise except that made by the lapwing and the curlew, or the occasional tinkling of a sheep-bell. Otherwise silence and deep peace brood over these high, cool districts. For him who would like to pursue these paths, there is a green world open.

THE BEAUTY THAT WAS
THE WINDMILL

A WINDMILL GROWS an ever rarer sight, and it is often rather a sorrowful one, since it is preserved only as a monument, part of the tradition of a vanished past, and no wind sets its sails whirling. Many a village still possesses a Mill Lane, but there is seldom a mill in it. If the jolly miller who lived on the River Dee were to walk at night the countryside, he would be horrified to find that in the whole of England there are now but forty windmills working, and several of them are on their last legs.

In the last two-and-twenty years the number of mills in one county, Suffolk, has come down from thirty-nine to five. It is sad, if inevitable, but at any rate if we can now too seldom see windmills, we can see at the Victoria and Albert Museum an exhibition of paintings, photographs and models of them, some still existing and some that are no more. They made an appeal to some of our most beloved artists: to Constable, the son of a miller who owned watermills at Flatford and Dedham and two windmills near East Bergholt; to Crome and Cotman, to mention but three illustrious names. Indeed there was a time when a mill was a normal charming part of any rural English landscape. If the mills themselves must gradually expire we shall at least always know how lovely they were.

> "IF THE MILLS THEMSELVES MUST GRADUALLY EXPIRE WE SHALL AT LEAST ALWAYS KNOW HOW LOVELY THEY WERE"

JULY 30TH, 1921

PLAYING BY THE SEA

OW WONDERFULLY PLEASANT the seaside would be to many of us if only we could approach it with the mind of a child. To a child the sea is enough itself. It is full of romance and excitement and of things to do. Alas! Many grown-ups have to admit that it is not so to them. For two days we can bask and loaf and blink drowsily at the sea – and then we grow bored. We must have a ball to hit or, at the very least, must look at someone else hitting one. There are others who can only think of the sea as something bordered by houses and hotels. They cannot imagine that there are in the world solitary stretches of coast or such a thing as a quiet seaside village where there is nothing in particular to do. I want a golf course and I despise the person who wants a promenade and a brass band, but really I do not think there is a penny to choose between us. We are equally contemptible – or pitiable.

Even the joy of climbing things is not so primitive a one as that of merely getting wet. Parents and nurses make churlish efforts to diminish this glory of wetness. They buy for their children voluminous pairs of bathing drawers, into which can be tucked an enormous quantity of clothing, giving to the wearer an agreeable and balloon-like appearance; but a kindly wavelet always comes sooner or later, just a little too high. Who does not know the look of the landing outside the nursery door in seaside lodgings? There are several small wet pairs of sand shoes, bathing garments tightly wrung out but still making little rivulets on the linoleum, and dank, crumpled pairs of stockings full of sand hung over the banisters.

AUGUST 24TH, 1940

THE ENGLISH SPIRIT

BY A. L. ROWSE

I T MAY SEEM presumptuous on the part of a Cornishman to write about the English spirit, yet there are things that a Cornishman can say which an Englishman perhaps could not. For one characteristic of the English is their very unselfconsciousness: they do not know what they are really like – a charming trait. The English think of themselves as a dull, plodding, humdrum, hardworking sort of people. They are nothing of the kind. So far from being hardworking, they are lazy, constitutionally indolent. They are always being caught lagging behind, unprepared; and then, when up against it – and not until they are up against it – they more than make up for lost time by their resourcefulness, their inventiveness, their ability to extemporise, their self-reliance.

At the core of the English spirit is happiness, a deep source of inner contentment with life, which explains the Englishman's profoundest wish, to be left alone, and his willingness to leave others to their own devices so long as they do not trouble his repose. I think we know where this spirit of happy contentment in life comes from: it comes from the particular relation, the secret compact that the Englishman has entered into with nature. Of all modern peoples it is the English who provide the best example of a people in harmony with their environment. That is why they are at ease at heart: none of that overstrain which makes the Germans such bad neighbours to everybody, so uncomfortable to themselves. The issue has become all the more momentous, the choice for the world between two totally different attitudes to life, between one spirit and the other, more clear.

I once asked a German friend of mine what was the specific quality among the English soldiers of the last war. His answer was surprising. He said "Their pride." When taken prisoner, battered, dirty, weary, wounded, their spirit was unbroken, they never dreamed of submission; they retained their self-respect, they assumed no other. The Germans were taken aback by this; they will have reason to be yet again. Everybody who met the men who came away from Dunkirk knows how completely unbroken their spirit was. Bombed to blazes, with no tanks and few planes, with their defences crumbling right and left, they were undismayed.

"THE SECRET COMPACT THAT THE ENGLISHMAN HAS ENTERED INTO WITH NATURE"

These things are unchanging in our history. It is perhaps at its highest moment of tension that the English spirit is most revealing of its nature. I find myself often in these days, when the R.A.F. is gradually wearing down the numerical superiority of Goering's air force, saying over to myself Howard's words to the Queen as he fought Philip's Armada all that week up the Channel: "By little, and by little, we pluck them of their feathers." It would serve as a motto for the Royal Air Force today.

That is the stuff of which the English spirit is made, no less than that dream of happiness and content which lies at the heart of every Englishman. Is it possible to think that such a spirit can ever be conquered?

FAMOUS OAKS OF ENGLAND

No country is richer than our own in magnificent oak trees. They are as much the peculiar glory of our land as the Alps are of Switzerland – they may fairly rank among the mightiest products of Nature. There are some still standing in England that may have successfully withstood all the storms and chances that have fought against them since the Norman Conquest! I have endeavoured to confer a sort of immortality upon the existing prize oaks of the country

> "THERE WILL REMAIN IN THE LAND THEY ADORNED SOME REMEMBRANCE OF THEIR ANCIENT SPLENDOUR"

by placing at least some image of them beyond the reach of evil chances. Lightning may blast them, winds may dismember them, rabbits may undermine them, schoolboys or gipsies may burn them, but at least there will remain in the land they adorned some remembrance of their ancient splendour. They have been silent witnesses of the vicissitudes of human history for many generations of men, and they seem to cast some of the scorn of time itself on the ephemeral pursuits and interests of humanity.

APRIL 23RD, 1921

THE LIFE OF THE FIELDS

APRIL IN THE old times was the month in which men were accustomed to go on pilgrimage. It still brings with it a kind of uneasiness and longing to leave the city for the fields, though spring is only at the stage when its heralds and premonitors are sent forth. They have come earlier than usual this year. The wild broom does not usually flower before the hawthorn, but this year we have found it already. It was in a bosky wood, sheltered on every side but the south.

One is inclined to think only the wild creatures are really beautiful in spring, but this would be doing a very great injustice to domestic animals. The silly sheep may not be much to look at in spring, nursing ewes are constantly hungry and have no care of their coats, which are ragged and torn with much scrambling through briar and thorn. But look at sheep in a flock and at a distance, and it will be strange if you do not find them fine figures in the landscape.

"THE SHEPHERD COUNTING HIS FLOCK AS THEY COME HOME TO REST IS A FIGURE OF NIGHT AND OF DREAMLAND"

The shepherd counting his flock as they come home to rest is a figure of night and dreamland. Who has not tried the ancient method of wooing Morpheus by counting the flock as it slips through a gate two or three at a time? To lose count and begin over again is of the very essence of the game.

FEBRUARY 12TH, 1910

THE SIMPLE LIFE

RECENTLY THERE HAS been much controversy in the daily Press as to what is the truth about the oft-repeated desire for a simple life expressed so freely during recent years. According to the cynical journalists a great deal is only poetry, and the most celebrated of our dramatists has said the best poetry is "the most feigning." He and the journalists are in agreement if the words be taken literally.

No doubt there is a good deal of feigning in the professions of love for a simple life. The majority naturally prefer the town. They like Nature on "the sweet shady side of Pall Mall." They are like the late Mr. Anthony Trollope and Mr. James Payne, whose favourite recreation was to play whist in the Reform Club. It is recorded that once upon a time they thought a visit to the country was necessary for their physical welfare, and so they adventured forth to a small town; but after a single walk

> "HE WHO LIVES COMPLETELY IN THE COUNTRY IS VERY APT TO GO TO RUST"

through the main street they returned to the station, waited for the next train, and did not feel happy until they were once more facing each other at dinner in the Reform Club. Probably there are more people like that than care to confess it. The wise man has told us that "no man quickeneth his own soul," and he who lives completely in the country is very apt to go to rust. To quote again, "Iron sharpeneth iron," and the anchorite is bound to grow dull for lack of intercourse with his intellectual equals.

239

AUGUST 24TH, 1940

THE NEW "MERRY ENGLAND"
VIEWS FROM A CHURCH TOWER
BY H. V. MORTON

I WAS STANDING on the tower of the village church the other night, gazing down upon a cluster of Saxon-looking cottages, thatched barns, cornfields and dark woods. Below me, at the foot of the belfry, lay the massive and unconscious forms of my comrades, I sunk in the slumber that comes to Home Guards who have been harvesting since dawn. A blessed sleep, a sleep that can deaden a man even to the sound of our belfry clock, which has a metallic fit every fifteen minutes, ending in a frustrated whirr of wheels; for we have stopped the chimes. From the parapet of the tower you can see nearly the whole of our parish. The Normans had built the church on what must have been a high clearing in a forest; now it is a bare ridge, with magnificent views all round, except to the immediate east, where the parish falls steeply into invisibility and dark woodland. Standing up there like some baron's man, brooding on these parish matters, it came to me that one of the most remarkable things about this war is the way

240

England has, for many us, ceased to be a country, or even a county, and has become a parish.

All over our land, villages, once proclaimed dead and done for, have awakened to arms. People, once hardly on speaking terms, have come together to organise defence. Danger has given us a common purpose. It has blown to a flame smouldering local loyalties and traditions. It has roused the English genius for improvisation. It has brought us face to face with the fact that we love our country well enough to die for her. Hitler has struck fine sparks from England: for this we owe him gratitude, for in the process of war we have touched old simplicities, and have known again the feeling that we belong to our country and our country to us.

> "FOR IN THE PROCESS OF WAR WE HAVE TOUCHED OLD SIMPLICITIES, AND HAVE KNOWN AGAIN THE FEELING THAT WE BELONG TO OUR COUNTRY"

Still, I confess that now and then, as I stand on guard, I relieve the weary hours with memories of those lovely places in England which I shall not see again until the war is over. Then my eye falls to the nearness of my own parish: to the group of ancient cottages, the thatched barns, the cornfields and dark woods. I, who once thought of England as a whole, and was in the habit of going to Cornwall or Cumberland on the spur of the moment, have not left my parish for months. Neither do I wish to do so; my parish has become England.

THE KISSING BOUGH OF ENGLAND

BY LAURENCE WHISTLER

CENTURIES BEFORE ANY Christmas tree was lit in this island there were English children at work on the Eve, binding evergreens, fastening little presents, and at last lighting the candles, on a device that evoked in them all the pleasure and excitement aroused by the tree in the Lutherans of Germany. They called it the Kissing Bough or the Kissing Bunch. It hung from the ceiling in a luminous crown: a hemisphere of evergreens marked with a ring of candles above, and with a ring of bright red apples below, curiously hinting at fulfilment in the hour of promise. And all this was only the frame to a bunch of mistletoe, suspended a little below the centre to explain the purpose and the name of the device.

So well liked was the Kissing Bough that it has never been entirely replaced by the tree. There are families in Derbyshire, Cheshire and Staffordshire, in Northumberland, and in Cornwall and Devon as well, who keep it to this day. The Bough is not always in the shape of a crown. It may take the form of a sphere or globe, and then the apples cluster in the centre, and the mistletoe hangs in a bunch underneath, where the circles cross. In the last century all manner of gay and glittering objects were added to the leaf-hidden frame: little robins, rabbits and squirrels, oranges and pears, stiff paper rosettes, bits of tinsel and bright-coloured ribbon, bits of looking-glass and Bethlehem stars cut out of shiny tin: And then the candles – set in a ring around the middle, or placed here and there about the frame.

On Christmas Eve those candles were lit and the Kissing Bough became the visible centre of the festival, lit again on the Day, and every evening thereafter till the Twelve Days were out. It hung from the middle of the ceiling, just high enough from the ground for a couple to stand or stoop and kiss beneath it. Every visitor to the house soon found his way to that point. It was there the carols were sung in a circle. It was there the Mummers held staggeringly forth, and arriving at the final act of their drama, they would all move forward to the Bough to bid farewell. It was indeed the crown and centre of Christmas. And the last kisses of the Eve were under those lights.

Kissing under the mistletoe is said to have been wholly an English custom, and we are reminded of the fame of England's kisses in late mediaeval and Tudor times. The foreign visitor thought it surprising – and rather pleasant; for the beauty of English women was proverbial, and where else but in England was a stranger not merely allowed but expected, not merely expected but invited, to greet his hostess and her daughters with a kiss on the lips? Now we do not embrace so easily in public – quite the reverse, in fact – but even today no girl is supposed to refuse a kiss when the mistletoe is above her, and, formerly, for every kiss that he took, a young man was entitled to put his hand in the circle of candles, and pull off one berry at a time.

"No good to call here." "Beware of the dog." "They will give food here." "You may get a job here."

"Three women here. Pitch a yarn." "They give you in charge here." "The Police arrest tramps here."